Thamer Alhazzaa

Saudi eBay Project: eBusiness, eCommerce and eAuction in Saudi Arabia

Development of an Online Auction Platform

GRIN Publishing

Bibliographic information published by the German National Library:

The German National Library lists this publication in the National Bibliography; detailed bibliographic data are available on the Internet at http://dnb.dnb.de .

Imprint:

Copyright © 2014 GRIN Verlag GmbH
Print and binding: Books on Demand GmbH, Norderstedt Germany
ISBN: 978-3-656-86281-9

This book at GRIN:

http://www.grin.com/en/e-book/285992/saudi-ebay-project-ebusiness-ecommerce-and-eauction-in-saudi-arabia

GRIN - Your knowledge has value

Since its foundation in 1998, GRIN has specialized in publishing academic texts by students, college teachers and other academics as e-book and printed book. The website www.grin.com is an ideal platform for presenting term papers, final papers, scientific essays, dissertations and specialist books.

Saudi eBay Project

Thamer F. Alhazzaa

Florida Institute of Technology

December 4, 2014

Author Note

Thamer F. Alhazzaa, School of Computing, College of Engineering, Florida Institute of

Technology.

This final report was required by XXX for the XXX Projects in Computer Information

Systems Capstone Course for the Fall 2014 semester.

Table of Contents

Abstract

The business world is rapidly changing. The principal reason of this persistent change is, without a doubt, the technology. Not only theoretically, by adding new terminologies to the business Wiki and archiving numerous financial eBooks on Kindle libraries, but also virtually, by flourishing small businesses and terminating other top market value ones, the Internet, in particular, has redefined the word 'business'.

eCommerce "Electronic Commerce" and eAuction "Electronic Auction" are just examples of the effects of the Internet on modern businesses and corporations. There are many reasons why both individuals and organizations conduct their businesses online these days. From an individual's perspective, convenience is one important reason why a college student who doesn't have a car may consider Amazon over Wal-Mart to purchase a new 55-inch T.V. Another reason is the ability to make comparisons among a wide range of similar products and competitor merchants. On the other hand, organizations have found a new market on the Internet. In fact, the competition has compelled them to find new opportunities online.

For this project, I have researched and investigated the reasons behind the slow eBusiness development in Saudi Arabia. Since an eGovernment program, Yesser Program, has already been started in Saudi Arabia, my concentration has been on the eCommerce portion and specifically on the eAuction topic to analyze whether or not there is an opportunity to start a Saudi version of eBay.

Keywords: eBusiness, eCommerce, eGovernment, eAuction, B2C, B2B, C2C.

Introduction

An auction is a process of trading products or services by offering them up for bidding, taking bids, and then selling the item to the highest bidder. It is a traditional kind of business by which people usually sell and/or buy used products. Buyers usually go to the auctions seeking low prices, whereas sellers normally resort to auctions to get rid of something that cannot be sold elsewhere.

Because of the drastic development of the technology and the convenience that the Internet provides, people have started to utilize the online services to do almost everything. At the forefront of these services are the business transactions. People these days seldom go to bank branches and prefer to use their mobile applications to do their businesses. eAuction is another example of business models that have become incredibly popular and preferred to the traditional ones due to the convenience that people have found on the Internet.

Background

eBay Inc., (stylized as eBay), is an American multinational corporation and eCommerce company that was founded by Pierre Omidyar in September 1995. eBay is one of the world's largest personal online trading communities. It created a new market: efficient one-to-one trading in an auction format on the Internet. eBay is headquartered in San Jose, California, and its mission, according to eBay, is to help people trade practically anything on earth.

As mentioned on eBay's website, individuals—not big businesses—use eBay to trade items in numerous categories, including collectibles, antiques, sports memorabilia, computers, toys, beanie babies, dolls, figures, coins, stamps, books, magazines, music, pottery, glass, photography, electronics, jewellery, gemstones, and much more.

As the leading Consumer-to-Consumer (C2C) trading website, buyers are attracted to eBay because of the large amount of content available, the competitive prices that cannot be found elsewhere, and the security and the privacy that eBay offers. Likewise, sellers use eBay due to the huge number of buyers obtainable and the straightforward process by which eBay is characterized.

eBusiness, eCommerce, and eGovernment

Electronic Business, or eBusiness, refers to the use of the technology and the Internet to perform the major business processes in an organization. According to K. Laudon and J. Laudon (2012), eBusiness includes activities for the internal management of an organization, processes for the coordination with suppliers and other partners, and actions for dealing with the commerce part of the business, the eCommerce.

eCommerce, on the other hand, is the portion of eBusiness that deals with the commercial activities. eCommerce encompasses not only buying and selling of goods and services over the Internet but also other activities supporting those market transactions, such as advertising, marketing, customer support, security, delivery, and payment.

eGovernment, as stated by K. Laudon and J. Laudon (2012), is the application of the technology to digitally allow governments and public sector agencies deliver information and services to citizens, businesses, and other arms of governments. eGovernment makes governmental operations more efficient and also empowers citizens by giving them easier access to information and effective ways to network electronically with public agencies and other citizens.

Types of eCommerce

One way to classify eCommerce transactions is by looking at the nature of the participants in them. The three major eCommerce categories are (K. Laudon & J. Laudon, 2012, p. 381):

Business-to-Consumer (B2C). B2C eCommerce includes selling products and services to individual shoppers. BarnesandNoble.com, which sells books, software, and music to individual consumers, is an example of B2C eCommerce.

Business-to-Business (B2B). B2B eCommerce includes sales of products and services among businesses. ChemConnect's website for buying and selling chemicals and plastics is an example of B2B eCommerce.

Consumer-to-Consumer (C2C). C2C eCommerce includes consumers selling directly to consumers. eBay, the giant eAuction website that enables people to sell their goods to other consumers by auctioning their merchandise off to the highest bidder or for a fixed price, and Craigslist, the most widely used platform used by consumers to buy from and sell directly to others, are great examples of C2C eCommerce.

Market Creator

Establish an eAuction platform similar to eBay, I should explain what the term 'Market Creator' means, and how it is related to the eCommerce. Market creators, according to K. Laudon and J. Laudon (2012), are the third parties that build digital environments in which buyers and sellers can meet, display products, search for products, and establish prices. eAuction markets like eBay and Priceline are good examples of the market creator business model. Another example is Amazon's Merchants platform where merchants are allowed to set up stores on Amazon's website and sell goods at fixed prices to consumers.

eAuction

eAuction is an eBusiness model between auctioneers and bidders that takes place over the Internet. The auctioneers offer their products, commodities, or services on a web-based auction system. Interested parties can submit their bid for the products to be auctioned in certain specified periods. The auction is transparent that all interested parties are allowed to participate in the auction in a timely manner. eAuction is an eCommerce system that can be in B2C, B2B, or C2C model. The two major types of eAuction are the 'forward auction' in which several bidders bid for one auctioneer's goods and the 'reverse auction' in which several auctioneers bid for one buyer's order.

Research Methodologies

To analyze the requirements of my Saudi eBay project, I used two methodologies to do my investigation and research. First, since my concentration in this project is on the Saudi online market, I have interviewed with some Saudi students and asked them about their experience with eBay, Craigslist, and Amazon. We discussed how their online purchases have changed since they moved to the United States. We have also negotiated the reasons why Saudi people who live in Saudi Arabia prefer to go shopping traditionally to do shopping online, whereas Saudi students, for instance, who live abroad do the reverse. All my interviewees and I agreed that one major reason is behind these two different Saudis' behaviors toward online shopping. After we all agreed that the Saudi Post has remarkably developed the mail services, we concluded that the lack of having a stable and fully featured website that is administrated and managed by Saudi cadre is the cause of this difference. I tried to gather information about the stable and fully featured website my interviewees believe its required for our market, so I can analyze the requirements of my project.

The second methodology was to read about the eCommerce systems, in general, and the eAuction ones, in particular, to understand the features of these systems. I spent a plenty of time browsing the content of eBay website and reading some articles about its extraordinary features in order to obtain an overall background about its system.

Findings, Analysis, and Discussions

Based on the previous investigation and research, I have found that the market is opened for a new eAuction system. People in Saudi Arabia, as in other nations, are willing to move to the web whenever they find an appropriate environment. Some of my interviewees have been using eBay and other eAuction websites not only for purchasing products but also for selling their unneeded ones. They believe that automated auctions have more advantages over the traditional ones. Advanced features such as searching for products and bidding history are not available for traditional auctioneers and bidders. Moreover, eAuction systems help traders avoid travel expenses and enable an easy way for them to do business both domestically and internationally.

This notwithstanding, eAuction systems have some limitations because of which eAuction cannot completely replace traditional auctions. The possibility of the fraud by either auctioneers or bidders, the hacking of the eAuction servers, and the identity and credit theft is a great example of the eAuction systems limitations. Furthermore, the incapability of having physical inspections of the products before purchasing them makes auctioning online on high-valued deals such as real estates impossible.

Conclusion and Recommendations

From the preceding investigation, I have reached a conclusion that there is a great opportunity to establish a new online trading or an eAuction system in Saudi Arabia. Interviewees' answers and ideas were very positive and encouraging. However, some of them had some concerns regarding the acceptance of the idea by people who never tried similar systems in Saudi Arabia. Thus, they recommended to start developing the project and targeting a small-scale audience to whom these kinds of systems are acquainted.

Furthermore, after I have precisely examined most of the extraordinary features that eBay robust system provides to its users, I have reached a fact that simulating such a great website is not an easy job. Developing a stable system with all these features requires a very long time of testing and enhancing.

I, therefore, decided to build a basic web-based application that provides the required online services that allow auctioneers and bidders to conduct business electronically. The Project Scope and Description and the Target Audiences sections describe the solution, its boundaries, and its audiences in more details.

Project Scope and Description

Saudi eBay is a web-based eAuction system that was coded using Java as a programming language (refer to the Tools and Technologies section for further details about the required software and tools). Saudi eBay provides a mechanism to perform the bidding process through which auctioneers and bidders can sell and buy products. The system has three key players, Saudi eBay administrators, auctioneers, and bidders. All players have their roles before, during, and after the auction process. These roles summarize the services that Saudi eBay system provides.

Target Audiences

The beta version of the Saudi eBay project targets the Florida Tech's Saudi Student Union (SSU) members. International students usually don't reside in one place for a long time. They usually move from a state to another looking for universities' acceptances. Consequently, students sometimes need to trade their furniture and equipment. As a member of the SSU, I have received a lot of emails from other members offering their furniture, automobiles, mobile phones, laptops, and other products. I believe that an automated system might be helpful for the students to avoid these inefficient practices, in my opinion. I have discussed the idea with the manager of the SSU, and I will work hard to develop a robust solution that meets all students' requirements.

After I develop the beta version of my project, I will share the website with the SSU members. All their opinions, ideas, suggestions, and comments will be valuable and absolutely considered important inputs to the development and enhancement plan of my project. My following goal will be extending my project's target audiences to involve all Saudi students in the United States.

Finally, based on the users' feedbacks and comments, I may add more features to the system, and I might Arabize the website and target all Saudi people including those who are not English speakers.

Algorithms / Project Solution

Saudi eBay is a 3-tier dynamic web-based application that allows three different categories of users, Admins, Auctioneers, and Bidders, to interact with the system through the following functionalities:

- Sellers can sign up as "Auctioneers".

- Auctioneers can upload, update, and delete products.

- Auctioneers can start auctions.

- Auctioneers can define the date range for bids.

- Auctioneers receive bids on their products.

- Auctioneers can award products to the highest bid. Otherwise, the system will award the product to the highest bid at the end of the Auction.

- Auctioneers can check sales history.

- Buyers can sign up as "Bidders".

- Bidders can browse products that are categorized in seven categories (Motors, Fashion, Electronics, Collectibles and Art, Home and Garden, Sporting and Goods, and Toys and Hobbies).

- Bidders can place bids on products.

- Winning Bidders make payments to the Auctioneers at the end of the auctions.

- Auctioneers receive payments and deliver products to the winning Bidders.

- Bidders can check purchases history.

- An Admin user can create other Admin users.

- An Admin user can edit, activate, deactivate, and delete other Admin users.

- An Admin user can edit, activate, and deactivate Auctioneers and Bidders.

- An Admin user can deactivate auctions.

- An Admin user can see statistics about transactions, sales, and purchases of products and

  can modify products that contain illegal information.

The following Use Case Diagram, Data Flow Diagram (DFD), Class Diagram, and

Entity-Relationship Diagram (ERD) respectively represent the functionalities, the data flow,

the structure, and the relationships among the entities of the Saudi eBay system (see figure 1,

figure 2, figure 3, and figure 4).

Use Case Diagram

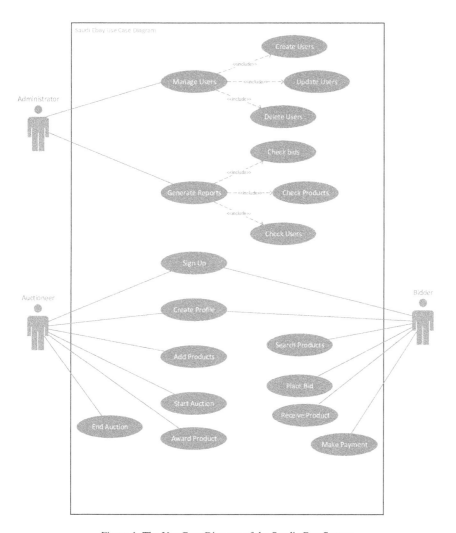

Figure 1. The Use Case Diagram of the Saudi eBay System.

Data Flow Diagram (DFD)

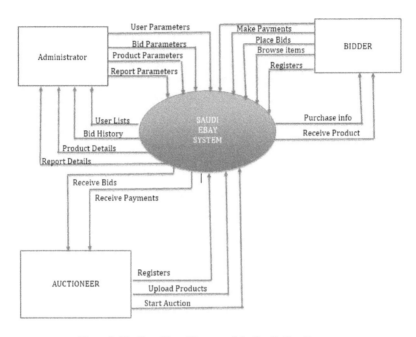

Figure 2. The Data Flow Diagram of the Saudi eBay System.

Class Diagram

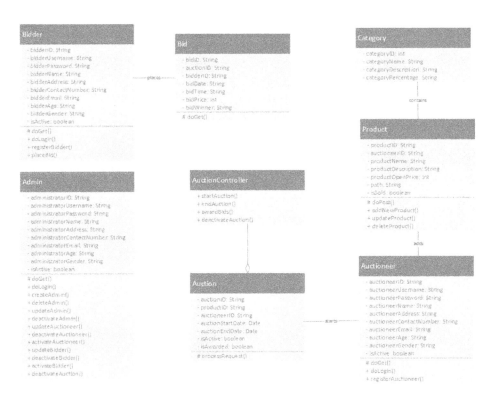

Figure 3. The Class Diagram of the Saudi eBay System.

Entity-Relationship Diagram (ERD)

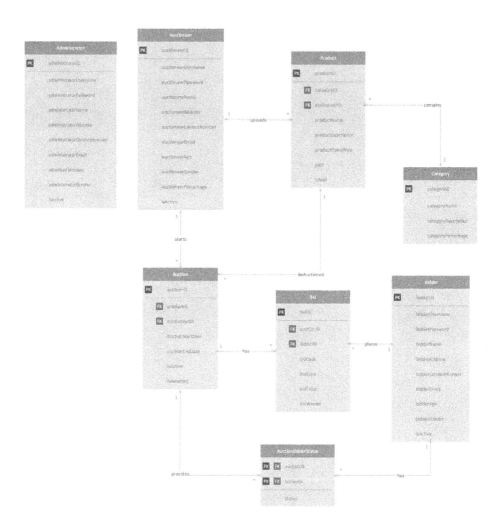

Figure 4. The Entity-Relationship Diagram of the Saudi eBay System.

Implementation

The development of the Saudi eBay project required specific set of software and tools.

The system was implemented using Java as a programming language, NetBeans as an IDE,

GlassFish as a web server, and Java DB as database. The Tools and Technologies section

discusses these tools and other technologies that were used to develop this project in more

details.

Tools and Technologies

This section describes in details all the specific resources that were used to implement the

Saudi eBay project.

- **Server Side Technologies:**

  o **Development Kit:** Java Development Kit (JDK) J2SE / JDK1.7 / J2EE

  To develop java-based applications, a developer needs to install the

  standard Java Development Kit (JDK) provided by Oracle Corporation for free at

  their official website. The JDK is one of the most widely used free development

  platform for developing platform-independent desktop-based and web-based

  applications. The output of java compiler is machine-readable byte code that is

  fast in executing and safe in embedding into systems. Moreover, Java is most

  famous in developing rich enterprise level web applications that are easy to

  deploy, run, and maintain. The war files generated by these applications can be

  transported easily to other servers.

  o **Integrated Development Environment (IDE):** NetBeans 8.0.2

  NetBeans is an advanced, rich, and also free IDE that is used for

  developing primarily with Java, but it is also used with other languages such as

PHP, C, C++, and HTML5. Netbeans is written in Java and can run on Windows,

OS X, Linux, Solaris, and other platforms supporting a compatible Java Virtual

Machine (JVM). NetBeans has built-in templates for web applications such as

static content, dynamic web content, and enterprise level applications. It provides

a clear overview of every java core library that a developer uses in an application.

- o **Web Server:** GlassFish 4.1

  GlassFish 4.1 is a lightweight and fast web server that is used to develop

  enterprise applications for small to medium size businesses. The Java DB

  database works better with the GlassFish server than other servers such as Apache

  Tomcat and WebLogic. It is also an open source product.

- o **Business Layer:** JSP, Servlets, JavaBeans, based on Model-View-Controller (MVC)

  JavaServer Pages (JSP) is a technology that helps software developers

  create dynamically generated web pages based on HTML, XML, or other

  document types. JSP is similar to PHP, but it uses Java programming language.

  To deploy and run JSPs, a compatible web server with a servlet container is

  required.

  Servlets are the Java platform technology of choice for extending and

  enhancing web servers. Servlets provide a component-based, platform-

  independent method for building web-based applications, without the

  performance limitations of CGI programs.

  JavaBeans is a technology that makes it easy to reuse software

  components. Developers can use software components written by others without

  having to understand their inner workings.

- **Client Side Technologies:**

  o **Client Layer (Front End):** HTML, CSS, JavaScript

    HyperText Markup Language (HTML), according to Boswell, is the primary markup language used to write content on the web. Every single web page on the Internet has at least some HTML markup included in its source code. HTML "tags" are words or acronyms surrounded by brackets. HTML tags are written as pairs; there must be a beginning tag and an ending tag in order to make the code display correctly.

    Cascading Style Sheets (CSS) is a new feature being added to HTML that gives both web site developers and users more control over how pages are displayed. With CSS, designers and users can create style sheets that define how different elements, such as headers and links, appear. These style sheets can then be applied to any web page. I used the CSS to format the web pages, add colors to them, and add layouts and different techniques to bring aesthetics to web pages.

    JavaScript is an interpreted programming or scripting language developed by Netscape to enable web authors to design interactive sites. JavaScript is used in web site development to do such things as automatically change a formatted date on a web page, cause a linked-to page to appear in a popup window, and cause text or a graphic image to change during a mouse rollover. I used JavaScript to validate text fields to make sure that correct data are passed to the server for processing. A server can also perform things that JavaScript does, but the reason behind using JavaScript is to prevent the server from doing extra tasks that JavaScript can do at the client side.

- **Database Management System (DBMS):**
    - o **Data Layer:** Java DB

        Java DB is a lightweight database that is provided by the standard Java

        installation. By using Java DB, there is no need to manage the database externally

        or independently from outside the development environment.

    - o **DDL and DML:** SQL (Structured Query Language)

        SQL is a special-purpose interactive and programming language designed

        for managing data held in a Relational Database Management System (RDBMS),

        Rouse (2005) said. SQL is the most widely used language as a Data Definition

        Language (DDL) and a Data Manipulation Language (DML). I used SQL to

        create tables, insert records in the tables, retrieve records from the tables, and

        update records in the tables via JDBC API (Java Database Connectivity).

- **Case Tools, Diagrams, and Project Plan**
    - o **Microsoft Visio Professional 2013:**

        The latest stable release of MS Visio 2013 is one of the best case tools

        applications available. It has thousands of templates and UML (Unified Modeling

        Language) diagrams in it, what makes it more advanced than other case tools

        available.

    - o **Microsoft Project Professional 2013:**

        Microsoft Project is a project management application that is designed to

        assist project managers, developers, and other planners in developing plans. The

        MS Project Professional 2013 was used to create a project plan for the Saudi eBay

        project and to produce a Gantt chart that explains the plan.

Development Schedule

This section provides a detailed development schedule describing all Saudi eBay

system's tasks and the time needed to finish each task. The schedule starts from the time when I

chose my project topic and ends with the final submission task (see table 1).

Week	Task	Description
1st Week August 18	Choosing the project topic	Providing the professor with at least two topics and sending an email that includes a brief info about the topics
2nd Week August 25	Confirming the topic and starting research	Confirming the project topic and preparing the first draft of the Project Proposal
3rd Week September 1	Completing the first draft of the Project Proposal	Providing the professor with the first draft of the Project Proposal for comments and approval
4th Week September 8	Development environment configuration	- Installing Java Development Kit, NetBeans IDE, Java DB database, Microsoft Windows inside VirtualBox virtual machine, Microsoft Visio 2013, and Microsoft Project 2013 - Testing the environment - Preparing for the first demonstration - Analyzing project requirements - Finalizing the final draft of the Project Proposal
5th Week September 15	Object-Oriented Analysis and Design (OOAD)	Requirements engineering, Use Cases, Data Flow Diagram, initial ER Diagram, Proposed Entities.
6th Week September 22	Database creation and testing connections	Creating the "Saudi_Ebay" database in the Java DB and test the connection with Java DB server.
7th Week September 29	Admin Module front-end design and business layer design	Starting creating the front-end design for the Admin Module and completing the business layer using server side coding.
8th Week October 6	Physical schema for Admin Module was created	Completing the tables for the Admin Module.

9th Week October 13	Connecting Admin Module with the database	The front-end of the Admin Module was connected to the database, and it was ready to receive inputs from the users.
10th Week October 20	Designing Auctioneer Module front-end, and physical schema for this module was created	The front-end of the Auctioneer module was designed, and relevant tables were created in database for the module.
11th Week October 27	Designing Bidder Module front-end, and physical schema for this module was created	The front-end of the Bidder module was designed, and relevant tables were created in database for the module.
12th Week November 3	Completing business layers for Auctioneer and Bidder Modules, and Connecting Modules with the database	Business layers were coded and connected to the database and inputs were given to it.
13th Week November 10	Enhancing the implementation of all modules	Checking all modules functionalities and preparing for the modules integration test.
14th Week November 17	Integration testing for all modules	All modules were connected with each other and reenactment was performed on them to make sure all modules work fine.
15th Week November 24	Finalizing the Final Report and cleaning the code	Finalizing the Final Report and cleaning the code.
16th Week December 1	Submitting all project's requirements	- Final report document - A zip file of source code - Third party API - A script to generate the database tables

Table 1. The Development Schedule of the Saudi eBay System.

Results and Lessons Learned

As planned at the beginning of this semester, a basic web-based application that provides the required online services that allow auctioneers and bidders to conduct business electronically was completely developed. The provided version of the Saudi eBay system provides a mechanism to perform the bidding process through which auctioneers and bidders can sell and buy products. The system has three key players, Saudi eBay administrators, auctioneers, and bidders. All players have their roles before, during, and after the auction process. These roles summarize the services that Saudi eBay system provides.

In an early stage of the project, I was planning to implement the system using different technologies, Visual Basic .NET as a programming language and Microsoft SQL Server as database. The reason behind that choice was to give myself a chance to try some development technologies that are different from those I have experienced during my graduate studies at Florida Tech. Consequently, I installed Microsoft Windows on a virtual machine on my MacBook, prepared a complete development environment, and started creating the database and the classes required to connect to it. However, since lots of Microsoft's development technologies have completely changed since the last time I used them, I found it difficult to adapt the new changes. I spent a plenty of time watching some tutorials and reading some books about web development using these technologies, but I recognized that I was running behind the schedule. Therefore, I decided to change my plan entirely by updating my project proposal with the new technologies, removing the old development environment, and preparing the new environment. I explained the situation to Dr. Parenteau, and we both discussed the proposal again and agreed that the time was apposite for change.

References

Boswell, W. (n.d.). HTML. *About Technology*. Retrieved September 10, 2014, from

http://websearch.about.com/od/h/g/html.htm

Deitel, P. J., & Deitel, H. M. (2012). *Java: how to program* (9th ed.). Upper Saddle River, N.J.: Prentice Hall.

Laudon, K., & Laudon, J. (2012). *Management Information Systems*. (12 ed.). Upper Saddle River, New Jersey: Prentice Hall.

Rouse, M. (2005, September 1). SQL (Structured Query Language). *TechTarget*. Retrieved September 10, 2014, from http://searchsqlserver.techtarget.com/definition/SQL

Appendix A

Software Configuration

This section provides all steps necessary to install, configure, and run the Saudi eBay project. A tester needs to go through all these steps in order to perfectly import and run the project. A tester also needs to look at and understand the Tools and Technologies section of this report to make sure that all required recourses are installed.

As mentioned in the Implementation section of this report, the Saudi eBay system was implemented using Java as a programming language, NetBeans as an IDE, GlassFish as a web server, and Java DB as database. NetBeans IDE 8.0.2 that is available at https://netbeans.org/ is a complete test environment for the Saudi eBay project. A tester can choose the proper Operating System platform from a drop-down list and then download and install the IDE bundle. If NetBeans was used as an IDE to test the Saudi eBay system, the "All" bundle that includes GlassFish Server Open Source Edition 4.1 would be a minimum requirement to run the system. Even though other IDEs such as Eclipse can be used to test the system, I really recommend using NetBeans.

After preparing the test environment, NetBeans on Mac OS X platform in this manual, a tester needs to import the provided Saudi_eBay.zip file into the IDE. Figure A1 below shows how to do this step. Moreover, a tester needs to add the provided third party API (ThirdPartyApi.zip) to the class path. A tester, first, needs to unzip this file that contains two APIs. One is the Commons FileUpload package that makes it easy to add robust, high-performance, file upload capability to Java Servlets and web applications. The second API is the Commons IO, which is a library of utilities to assist with developing IO functionality. A tester can import APIs files to the class path by right clicking on the Saudi_eBay project and going to

Properties (see figure A2). After that, a tester needs to click on Libraries, make sure that Compile

tab is selected, and then click on Add JAR/Folder (see figure A3). Both files must be selected

and checked before clicking "OK" (see figure A4 and figure A5).

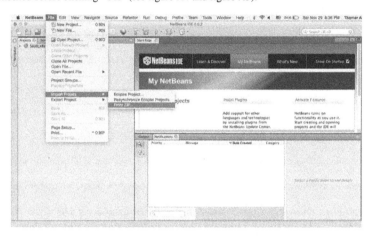

Figure A1. Import the Saudi eBay Project from ZIP.

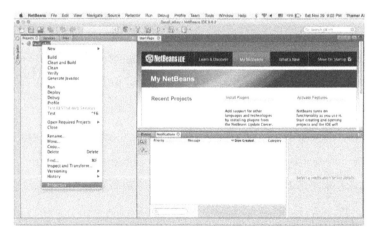

Figure A2. Saudi eBay Project Properties.

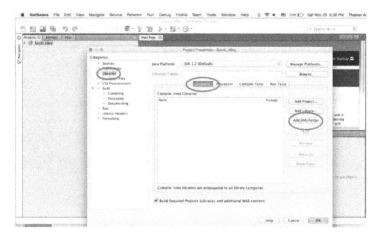

Figure A3. Edit Saudi_eBay Project Properties.

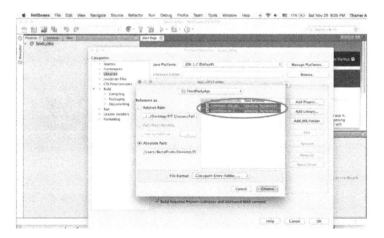

Figure A4. Both APIs Must Be Selected.

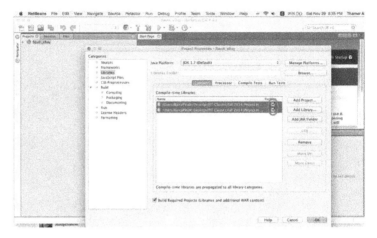

Figure A5. Both APIs Must Be Checked.

After finishing importing the Saudi_eBay project and the required APIs, a tester, now,

needs to create the Saudi_eBay database. Creating the database, a tester needs to follow the

following steps:

1. Click on Services tab and then expand the Databases menu (see figure A6)

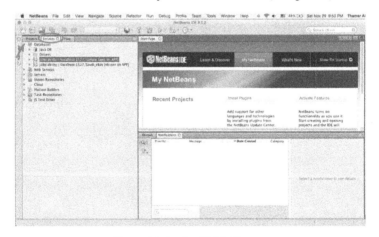

Figure A6. Services Tab is Chosen.

2. Right click on Java DB and then click on "Create Database" (see figure A7).

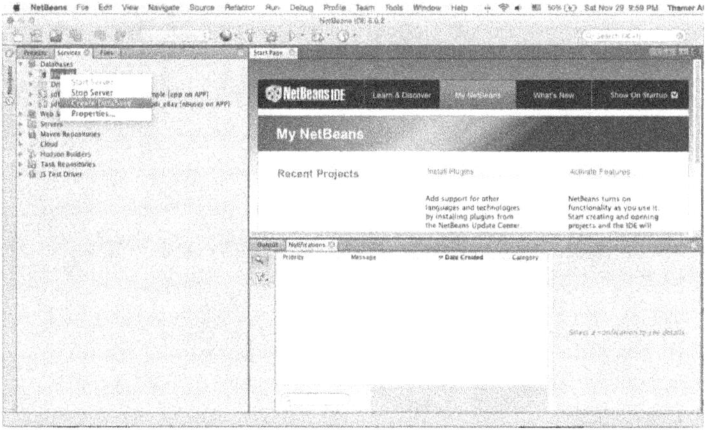

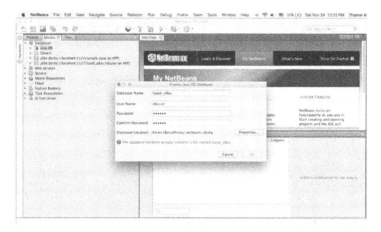

Figure A7. Create Java DB Database.

3. Type "Saudi_eBay" as the Database Name and "nbuser" as both the User Name

and the Password. Please note that these details are case sensitive (see figure A8).

Figure A8. Create Java DB Database.

4. Now, click on Java DB again and click on "Start Server" (see figure A9).

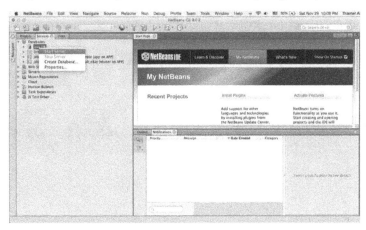

Figure A9. Start Java DB Server.

5. Click on Saudi_eBay and click "Connect" (see figure A10).

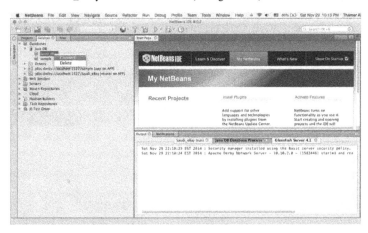

Figure A10. Connect Saudi_eBay Database.

6. Expand the Other schemas, right click on the APP, and then click on "Set as

Default Schema".

A tester is now done with creating the Saudi_eBay Database. He/She, then, needs to

create the database tables. The following steps explain how to create the required tables using

SQL commands:

1. After APP schema is set as default schema, expand APP, right click on Tables, and then

   click on "Execute Command" (see figure A11).

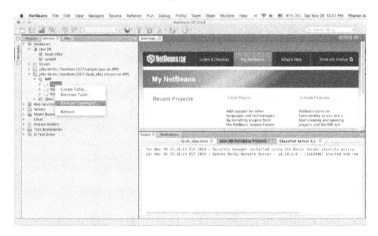

Figure A11. Execute SQL Commands to Create Database Tables.

2. A query window will be opened in the Editor Region of NetBeans. Now, start

   pasting the provided SQL commands in the "Saudi_eBay Database Queries.txt"

   file and run them one by one by clicking on "Run SQL" (see figure A12). Make

   sure to run the SQL commands in the same order as they are in the provided file.

Figure A12. Execute SQL Commands to Create Database Tables.

3. After all database tables are created, two tables, Administrator table and Category

table, need to be provided with some records. First, a single record needs to be

inserted into the Administrator table. This record represents the "Saudi eBay

Super Administrator" in the database. This step can be done by first right click on

Administrator table and then click on "View Data" (see figure A13).

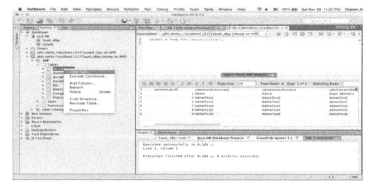

Figure A13. View Data of Administrator Table.

4. Now, right click anywhere on the window below the query wizard that is opened

after viewing data from Administrator table and then click on "Insert Record(s)"

(see figure A14).

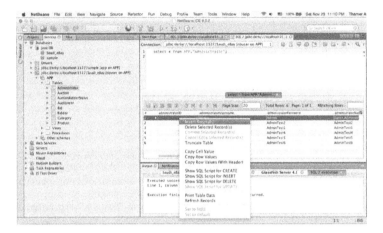

Figure A14. Insert Super Administrator Record into Administrator Table.

5. Double click on the administratorUsername field and type "Admin" then tab to

the administratorPassword field and type "Admin". Please note that these details

are case sensitive. Also, do not touch administratorID field, as it is auto generated.

Click OK to insert the Super Administrator record (see figure A15).

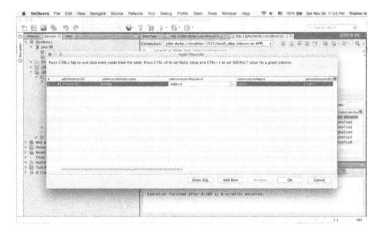

Figure A15. Insert Super Administrator Record.

6. Now, Category table needs to be updated with seven records that represent the predefined categories of the Saudi eBay products. To do this step, repeat the same steps done to insert a record into Administrator table and use the same records shown in figure A16 following the same order. Make sure that categoryIDs are auto generated as they are, and please note that categoryName field is case sensitive.

#	categoryID	categoryName	categoryDescription	categoryPercentage
1	1 motors	motors	motors	motors
2	2 fashion	fashion	fashion	fashion
3	3 electronics	electronics	electronics	electronics
4	4 collectibles	collectibles	collectibles	collectibles
5	5 home	home	home	home
6	6 sporting	sporting	sporting	sporting
7	7 toys	toys	toys	toys

Figure A16. Category Table Records.

Now, Saudi_eBay project is ready to run. Right click on Saudi_eBay and then click on

"Run" (see figure A17). NetBeans, then, will automatically open the login page of the system on

the chosen web browser (see figure A18). Saudi eBay system is compatible with Google

Chrome, Firefox, Safari, and Internet Explorer. I highly recommend updating the web browser to

the latest version before running the system.

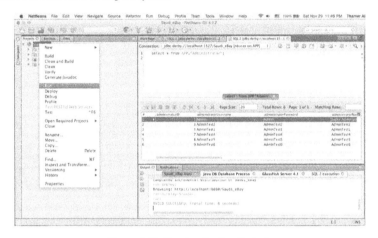

Figure A17. Run Saudi_eBay Project.

Figure A18. Saudi_eBay Login Page.

Appendix B

User's Manual

This section provides all instructions for Saudi eBay's users (Administrators, Auctioneers, and

Bidders) to run the system and perform all functionalities once the system has been installed.

This User's Manual is divided to three parts. Each part covers all instructions needed by a

particular kind of users (Administrators, Auctioneers, or Bidders).

Administrator Module

The Super Saudi eBay Administrator can access the system by entering his/her

credentials in the Username and Password fields of the "Administrator's login page" and then

clicking on "Submit" (see figure B1). Other Administrators can login to the system using the

same login page, yet they need to be created first by the Super Administrator or other predefined

Administrators. Instructions of how to create a new Administrator are explained later in this part.

Figure B1. Administrators' Login Page.

The system then directs Administrators to their "Home page". By moving the cursor on

"Menu", an Administrator can see all functionalities provided to manage the system. An

Administrator also can logout from the system at any time from any page by clicking on

"Logout". Moreover, an Administrator can return to the "Home page" at any time from any page

by clicking on "Home" (see figure B2).

Figure B2. Administrators' Panel.

To create a new Saudi eBay Administrator, an Administrator clicks on "Create an

Admin". The Administrator then needs to fill in all required details of the new Administrator and

clicks on "Submit" (see figure B3). If any field is missing, a prompt message appears requiring

the Administrator to complete all required details (see figure B4).

To edit Saudi eBay Administrators' details, an Administrator clicks on "Edit Admins"

(see figure B5). From this page, an Administrator can activate, deactivate, delete, and edit all

Saudi eBay Administrators except the Super Administrator. The Super Administrator, on the

other hand, can manipulate all other Administrators without any limitations.

Figure B3. Create a New Administrator.

Figure B4. A Field is Missing.

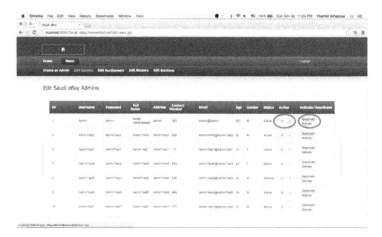

Figure B5. Edit Administrators.

To edit Saudi eBay Auctioneers' details, an Administrator clicks on "Edit Auctioneers"

(see figure B6). From this page, an Administrator can activate, deactivate, and edit all Saudi

eBay Auctioneers.

Figure B6. Edit Auctioneers.

To edit Saudi eBay Bidders' details, an Administrator clicks on "Edit Bidders" (see

figure B7). From this page, an Administrator can activate, deactivate, and edit all Saudi eBay

Bidders.

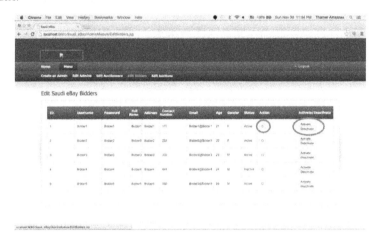

Figure B7. Edit Bidders.

To edit Saudi eBay Auctions, an Administrator clicks on "Edit Auctions" (see figure B8).

From this page, an Administrator can see all details of the "activate" auctions on the system. The

Administrator also can click on "Deactivate Auction" button below the auction's details to

deactivate that particular auction.

Figure B8. Edit Auctions.

Auctioneer Module

A new Auctioneer can register through the "New Auctioneer Registration" page. To go to this page, the new Auctioneer clicks on "Register as an Auctioneer" from the home page of the Saudi eBay website (see figure B9). Registered Auctioneers, on the other hand, can sign in and access the system through the Auctioneers' login page. To go to this page, registered Auctioneers click on "Sign in as an Auctioneer" from the home page (see figure B9).

Figure B9. Sign-up and Sign-in as an Auctioneer.

To register as an Auctioneer, the new user needs to complete all fields of the new Auctioneer registration form and then click on "Submit" (see figure B10).

Figure B10. New Auctioneer Registration.

An Auctioneer can access the system by entering his/her credentials in the Username and Password fields of the "Auctioneers' login page" and then clicking on "Submit" (see figure B11).

Figure B11. Auctioneers' Login Page.

The system then directs Auctioneers to their "Home page". By moving the cursor on "Menu", an Auctioneer can see all functionalities provided to manage the system. An Auctioneer also can logout from the system at any time from any page by clicking on "Logout". Moreover, an Auctioneer can return to the "Home page" at any time from any page by clicking on "Home" (see figure B12).

Figure B12. Auctioneers' Panel.

Now, to add a new product, an Auctioneer clicks on "Add Product", provides all required

information including an image for the product, and then clicks on "Submit" (see figure B13).

Figure B13. Add a New Product.

The system then directs the Auctioneer to the "Product Summary" page. From this page,

the Auctioneer can check all provided information of the new-added product (see figure B14).

Figure B14. Product Summary Page.

To see all added products, an Auctioneer clicks on "My Products" from the main menu.

From this page, the Auctioneer can edit a product, delete it, or start an auction on it by clicking

on "Edit Product", "Delete Product", or the image of the product respectively (see figure B15).

Please note that an Auctioneer cannot either edit or delete a product for which he/she has already

started an auction. In order to do that, the Auctioneer needs to contact System Administrators via

email.

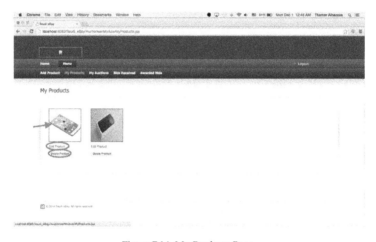

Figure B14. My Products Page.

When the Auctioneer clicks on the image of the product, the system directs him/her to

page from which the Auctioneer can start the auction. To start the auction, the Auctioneer needs

to provide valid dates for both the "Auction Start Date" and the "Auction End Date" fields and

then click on "Start Auction" button (see figure B15). Failure to provide valid information will

result in directing the Auctioneer to an error page that asking to go back and provide correct

information (see figure B16).

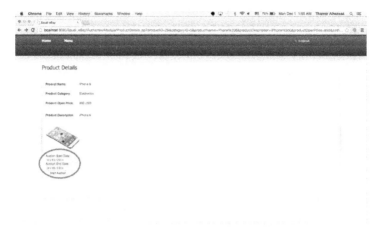

Figure B15. Start an Auction Page.

Figure B16. Valid Dates Prompt Page.

To see all active auctions, an Auctioneer clicks on "My Auctions" from the main menu.

From this page, the Auctioneer can see all active auctions with all their details (see figure B17).

Figure B17. My Auctions Page.

To see the bids received on their auctions, Auctioneers click on "Bids Received" from the

main menu. From this page, Auctioneers can see their active auctions with all details (see figure

B18). To see the bids received on a product, the Auctioneer needs to click on the image of that

particular product. The system then directs the Auctioneer to a new page (see figure B19) that

shows all bids received on his/her product with "Award Highest Bid" button on top of those bids

to allow the Auctioneer to "manually" sell the product to the highest Bidder if the Auctioneer

wants to sell his/her product immediately and prefers not to wait until the end time of the

auction, which is 11:59:59 P.M. of the selected "Auction End Date", the time at which the

system "automatically" awards the product to highest Bidder. When the Auctioneer clicks on the

"Award Highest Bid" button, the system directs him/her to the "Awarded Bids" page, which also

can be reached by clicking on "Awarded Bids" from main menu (see figure B20). This page

shows all awarded products with their details and pictures. To see the winning bid information of

product, the Auctioneer clicks on image of that particular product to be directed to a new page

with the desired information (see figure 21).

Figure B18. Bids Received Page.

Figure B19. Bids Received on a Product.

Figure B20. Awarded Bids Page.

Figure B21. The Winner Bid Information Page.

Bidder Module

A new Bidder can register through the "New Bidder Registration" page. To go to this

page, the new Bidder clicks on "Register as a Bidder" from the home page of the Saudi eBay

website (see figure B22). Registered Bidders, on the other hand, can sign in and access the

system through the Bidders' login page. To go to this page, registered Bidders click on "Sign in

as a Bidder" from the home page (see figure B22).

Figure B22. Sign-up and Sign-in as a Bidder.

To register as a Bidder, the new user needs to complete all fields of the new Bidder

registration form and then click on "Submit" (see figure B23).

Figure B23. New Bidder Registration.

A Bidder can access the system by entering his/her credentials in the Username and

Password fields of the "Bidders' login page" and then clicking on "Submit" (see figure B24).

Figure B24. Bidders' Login Page.

The system then directs Bidders to their "Home page". By moving the cursor on "Menu",

a Bidder can see all functionalities provided to manage the system. A Bidder also can logout

from the system at any time from any page by clicking on "Logout". Moreover, a Bidder can

return to the "Home page" at any time from any page by clicking on "Home" (see figure B25).

Figure B25. Bidders' Panel.

Now, to browse auctioned products, a Bidder clicks on "Browse Products" from the main

menu. The system then directs the Bidder to the Saudi eBay products' categories page (see figure

B26), the page from which the Bidder can click on the desired category to browse its products.

Figure B26. Products' Categories Page.

When the Bidder clicks on the desired category, the system shows all available products

on that particular category with all products' details (see figure B27).

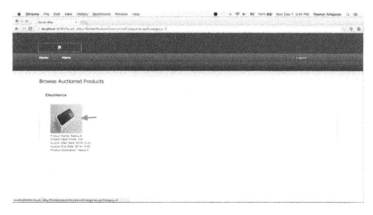

Figure B27. Electronics Category's Auctioned Products.

To place a bid on a product, the Bidder needs to click on the image of the product to be directed to the "Place a Bid" page where the Bidder can see all details of the product and the auction on it including the "Product Open Price" and the "Highest Bid" if there is one. This page also contains a text field to allow the Bidder to enter his/her bid amount and a button on which the Bidder should click to submit his/her bid (see figure 28). The bid amount must be greater than the "Product Open Price" and the "Highest Bid" if there is one. Otherwise, an error message is shown prompting the Bidder to go back and enter a valid bid (see figure 29).

Figure B28. Place a Bid Page.

Figure B29. A Valid Bid Prompt Page.

After placing a valid bid, the Bidder is directed to the "My Bids" page, which also can be

reached by clicking on "My Bids" from main menu (see figure B30). From this page, Bidders

can see all their placed bids with all their details. Another important information about placing

valid bids is that a Bidder cannot place "consecutive bids" on one product. If that happened, an

error message would be shown informing the Bidder that he/she cannot place another bid (see

figure B31).

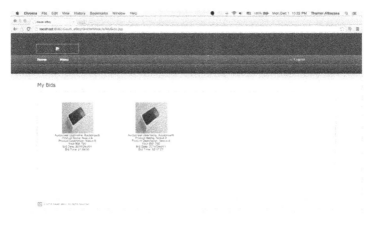

Figure B30. My Bids Page.

Figure B31. Consecutive Bids Error.

Finally, to see his/her winning bids, a Bidder can click on "My Winning Bids" from the

main menu to be directed to a new page that shows all his/her winning bids with the products and

bids details (see figure B32).

Figure B32. My Winning Bids Page.

Appendix C

Source Code

```
/*
 * Saudi eBay Project
 * Last Modified: Mon Nov 17, 2014 6:00 PM
 * The ConnectToDb class is a DAO (Data Access Object)
 * It is used to connect to the Saudi_eBay database and provide usability in other classes
 */

package org.saudiebay.dbaccess;
// import statements
import java.sql.Connection;
import java.sql.DriverManager;
import java.sql.SQLException;

// class ConnectToDb
public class ConnectToDb
{

    // database URL, username, and password declarations
    static final private String DATABASE_URL = "jdbc:derby://localhost:1527/Saudi_eBay";
    static final private String USERNAME = "nbuser";
    static final private String PASSWORD = "nbuser";

    private Connection connection = null;

    // connectToDb method to return a Connection
    public Connection connectToDb()
    {
        // try to connect to the Saudi_eBay database
        try
        {
            connection = DriverManager.getConnection(DATABASE_URL, USERNAME,
PASSWORD);
        }
        catch (SQLException e)
        {
            System.out.println(e.getLocalizedMessage());
        }

        return connection; // return a Connection
    } // end connectToDb method

} // end ConnectToDb class
```

```
/*
 * Saudi eBay Project
 * Last Modified: Mon Nov 17, 2014 6:00 PM
 * Admin class is used by Saudi eBay Admins to login, create new Admins, delete existing
Admins,
 * update existing Admins, activate and deactivate Admins, update, activate, and deactivate
Bidders,
 * and update, activate, and deactivate Auctioneers.
 */

package org.saudiebay.adminmodule;

// import statements
import java.io.IOException;
import java.sql.Connection;
import java.sql.ResultSet;
import java.sql.Statement;
import javax.servlet.ServletException;
import javax.servlet.http.HttpServlet;
import javax.servlet.http.HttpServletRequest;
import javax.servlet.http.HttpServletResponse;
import javax.servlet.http.HttpSession;
import org.saudiebay.dbaccess.ConnectToDb;

// class Admin
public class Admin extends HttpServlet
{
    // variables declaration
    private Connection connection;
    private Statement statement;
    private ResultSet resultSet;

    private String administratorID;
    private String administratorUsername;
    private String administratorPassword;
    private String administratorName;
    private String administratorAddress;
    private String administratorContactNumber;
    private String administratorEmail;
    private String administratorAge;
    private String administratorGender;

    /**
     * Processes requests for both HTTP <code>GET</code> and <code>POST</code>
     * methods.
     *
```

```
 *  @param request servlet request
 *  @param response servlet response
 *  @throws ServletException if a servlet-specific error occurs
 *  @throws IOException if an I/O error occurs
 */
// method doGet
@Override
protected void doGet(HttpServletRequest request, HttpServletResponse response) throws
ServletException, IOException
{
    response.setContentType("text/html;charset=UTF-8");

    if (request.getParameter("deactivateauctioneer") != null)
    {
        String auctioneerID = request.getParameter("auctioneerID");
        deactivateAuctioneer(request, response, auctioneerID);
    }

    if (request.getParameter("activateauctioneer") != null)
    {
        String  auctioneerID = request.getParameter("auctioneerID");
        activateAuctioneer(request, response, auctioneerID);
    }
    if (request.getParameter("deactivatebidder") != null)
    {
        String bidderID = request.getParameter("bidderID");
        deactivateBidder(request, response, bidderID);
    }
    if (request.getParameter("activatebidder") != null)
    {
        String bidderID = request.getParameter("bidderID");
        activateBidder(request, response, bidderID);
    }

    if (request.getParameter("adminlogin") != null)
    {
        // receiving username and password from AdminLogin.jsp form
        administratorUsername = request.getParameter("administratorUsername");
        administratorPassword = request.getParameter("administratorPassword");

        doLogin(request, response, administratorUsername, administratorPassword);
    }

    if (request.getParameter("createnewuser") != null)
    {
        // receiving new Admin parameters from AdminPanel.jsp form
```

```
administratorUsername = request.getParameter("administratorUsername");
administratorPassword = request.getParameter("administratorPassword");
administratorName = request.getParameter("administratorName");
administratorAddress = request.getParameter("administratorAddress");
administratorContactNumber = request.getParameter("administratorContactNumber");
administratorEmail = request.getParameter("administratorEmail");
administratorAge = request.getParameter("administratorAge");
administratorGender = request.getParameter("administratorGender");

        createAdmin(request, response, administratorUsername, administratorPassword,
administratorName, administratorAddress, administratorContactNumber, administratorEmail,
administratorAge, administratorGender);
}

    if (request.getParameter("deleteuser") != null)
    {
        administratorID = request.getParameter("administratorID");
        deleteAdmin(request, response, administratorID);
    }

    if (request.getParameter("updateuser") != null)
    {
        administratorID = request.getParameter("administratorID");
        String administratorID2 = request.getParameter("administratorID2");
        administratorUsername = request.getParameter("administratorUsername");
        administratorPassword = request.getParameter("administratorPassword");
        administratorName = request.getParameter("administratorName");
        administratorAddress = request.getParameter("administratorAddress");
        administratorContactNumber = request.getParameter("administratorContactNumber");
        administratorEmail = request.getParameter("administratorEmail");
        administratorAge = request.getParameter("administratorAge");
        administratorGender = request.getParameter("administratorGender");
        updateAdmin(request, response, administratorID, administratorUsername,
administratorPassword, administratorName, administratorAddress, administratorContactNumber,
administratorEmail, administratorAge, administratorGender, administratorID2);
    }

    if (request.getParameter("deactivate") != null)
    {
        administratorID = request.getParameter("administratorID");
        deactivateAdmin(request, response, administratorID);
    }

    if (request.getParameter("activate") != null)
    {
        administratorID = request.getParameter("administratorID");
```

```
      activateAdmin(request, response, administratorID);
   }

   if (request.getParameter("updateAuctioneerUser") != null)
   {
      String auctioneerID = request.getParameter("auctioneerID");
      String auctioneerUsername = request.getParameter("auctioneerUsername");
      String auctioneerPassword = request.getParameter("auctioneerPassword");
      String auctioneerName = request.getParameter("auctioneerName");
      String auctioneerAddress = request.getParameter("auctioneerAddress");
      String auctioneerContactNumber = request.getParameter("auctioneerContactNumber");
      String auctioneerEmail = request.getParameter("auctioneerEmail");
      String auctioneerAge = request.getParameter("auctioneerAge");
      String auctioneerGender = request.getParameter("auctioneerGender");
      updateAuctioneer(request, response, auctioneerID, auctioneerUsername,
auctioneerPassword, auctioneerName, auctioneerAddress, auctioneerContactNumber,
auctioneerEmail, auctioneerAge, auctioneerGender);
   }

   if (request.getParameter("updateBidderUser") != null)
   {
      // System.out.println("asdasd");
      String bidderID = request.getParameter("bidderID");
      String bidderUsername = request.getParameter("bidderUsername");
      String bidderPassword = request.getParameter("bidderPassword");
      String bidderName = request.getParameter("bidderName");
      String bidderAddress = request.getParameter("bidderAddress");
      String bidderContactNumber = request.getParameter("bidderContactNumber");
      String bidderEmail = request.getParameter("bidderEmail");
      String bidderAge = request.getParameter("bidderAge");
      String bidderGender = request.getParameter("bidderGender");
      updateBidder(request, response, bidderID, bidderUsername, bidderPassword,
bidderName, bidderAddress, bidderContactNumber, bidderEmail, bidderAge, bidderGender);
   }
} // end doGet method

// doLogin method
public void doLogin(HttpServletRequest request, HttpServletResponse response, String
administratorUsername, String administratorPassword) throws IOException
{
   String query = null;

   // creating an object for class AdminLoginAction
   AdminLoginAction adminLoginAction = new AdminLoginAction();

   try
```

```
{
    ConnectToDb db = new ConnectToDb();
    connection = db.connectToDb();

    // calling auhtenticate method and passing username and password to make sure that they
both are not empty
    boolean result = adminLoginAction.authenticate(administratorUsername,
administratorPassword);

    if (result)
    {
        // creating the sql query object
        statement = connection.createStatement();
        query = "select * from APP.\"Administrator\" where \"administratorUsername\" = '" +
administratorUsername + "' and \"administratorPassword\"= '" + administratorPassword + "'";

        // executing the query and storing the returned resultset
        resultSet = statement.executeQuery(query);

        if (resultSet.next())
        {
            query = "select * from APP.\"Administrator\" where \"administratorUsername\" = '"
+ administratorUsername + "' and \"administratorPassword\"= '" + administratorPassword + "'
and \"isActive\"= true";

            // executing the query and storing the returned resultset
            resultSet = statement.executeQuery(query);

            if (resultSet.next())
            {
                String userSessionID;
                statement.clearBatch();
                userSessionID = resultSet.getString(1);

                // creating a session
                HttpSession httpSession = request.getSession(true);
                httpSession.setAttribute("administratorID", userSessionID);

                // if the username and password entered are matched with those in table, the
response will be redirected to the AdminPanel
                response.sendRedirect("AdminModule/AdminPanel.jsp");
            }
            else
            {
                response.sendRedirect("AdminLogin.jsp?error=Username is Inactive. Contact
Super Administrator.");
```

```
                  }
                  }
                  else
                  {
                      // if either the username or the password is not correct, the response will be
            redirected to AdminLogin.jsp page with an error message
                          response.sendRedirect("AdminLogin.jsp?error=Wrong Username or Password.
            Please try again!");
                  }
                  }
                  else
                  {
                      response.sendRedirect("AdminLogin.jsp?error=Please fill in all required fields!");
                  }
              }
              catch(Exception e)
              {
                  System.err.println(e.getLocalizedMessage());
              }
          } // end doLogin method

          // createAdmin method
          public void createAdmin(HttpServletRequest request, HttpServletResponse response, String
          administratorUsername, String administratorPassword, String administratorName, String
          administratorAddress, String administratorContactNumber, String administratorEmail, String
          administratorAge, String administratorGender) throws IOException
          {
              // a server side fields validation to make sure that feilds are not left empty
              if (!administratorUsername.trim().equalsIgnoreCase("") &&
          !administratorPassword.trim().equalsIgnoreCase("")
                  && !administratorName.trim().equalsIgnoreCase("") &&
          !administratorAddress.trim().equalsIgnoreCase("")
                      && !administratorContactNumber.trim().equalsIgnoreCase("") &&
          !administratorEmail.trim().equalsIgnoreCase("")
                      && !administratorAge.trim().equalsIgnoreCase("") &&
          !administratorGender.trim().equalsIgnoreCase(""))
              {
                  try
                  {
                      // connecting to database
                      ConnectToDb connect = new ConnectToDb();
                      connection = connect.connectToDb();

                      // initializing an sql statement object
                      statement = connection.createStatement();
```

```
        // a query to check if the entered username or email already exist in the database
        String query = "select * from APP.\"Administrator\" where
\"administratorUsername\"='" + administratorUsername + "' or \"administratorEmail\"='" +
administratorEmail + "'";
        resultSet = statement.executeQuery(query); // executing the query

        // if the username or the email already exist in the Admin table
        if (resultSet.next())
        {
            // sending the redict to the CreateNewUser.jsp page with the message that the
username or the email already exist
            response.sendRedirect("AdminModule/CreateNewUser.jsp?msg=The entered
Username or email address is already taken. Please choose another Username or use another
email address!");
        }
        else
        {
            String command = "INSERT INTO
APP.\"Administrator\"(\"administratorUsername\",\"administratorPassword\",\"administratorNa
me\",\"administratorAddress\",\"administratorContactNumber\",\"administratorEmail\",\"adminis
tratorAge\",\"administratorGender\",\"isActive\") VALUES('" + administratorUsername + "','" +
administratorPassword + "','" + administratorName + "','" + administratorAddress + "','" +
administratorContactNumber + "','" + administratorEmail + "','" + administratorAge + "','" +
administratorGender + "',true)";
            statement.executeUpdate(command); // executing the sql command

            // sending the redirect to the CreateNewUser.jsp page with the message that A new
Administrator has successfully been created.
            response.sendRedirect("AdminModule/CreateNewUser.jsp?msg=A new
Administrator has successfully been created.");
        }

    }
    catch (Exception e)
    {
        System.err.println(e.getLocalizedMessage());
    }

    // release resources
    finally
    {
        try
        {
            if (resultSet != null)
            {
```

```
          resultSet.close();
        }
      }
      catch (Exception e)
      {
      }

      try
      {
        if (statement != null)
        {
          statement.close();
        }
      }
      catch (Exception e)
      {
      }

      try
      {
        if (connection != null)
        {
          connection.close();
        }
      }
      catch (Exception e)
      {
      }
    }
  }
  else
  {
    response.sendRedirect("AdminModule/CreateNewUser.jsp?msg=Please fill in all
required fields!");
  }
} // end createAdmin method

// method deleteAdmin
public void deleteAdmin(HttpServletRequest request, HttpServletResponse response, String
administratorID)
{
  try
  {
    // connecting to database
    ConnectToDb connect = new ConnectToDb();
    connection = connect.connectToDb();
```

```
// initializing an sql statement object
statement = connection.createStatement();

String query = "Select * from App.\"Administrator\" where \"administratorID\"=" +
administratorID;
resultSet = statement.executeQuery(query);


if (resultSet.next())
{
   String stringAdminID = resultSet.getString(1);
   int intAdminID = Integer.parseInt(stringAdminID);

   // Super Administrator cannot be deleted
   if (intAdminID == 1)
   {
       response.sendRedirect("AdminModule/EditUsers.jsp?msg=Super Administrator
cannot be deleted!");
   }
   else
   {
       String command = "Delete from App.\"Administrator\" where \"administratorID\"="
+ administratorID;
       statement.executeUpdate(command);
       response.sendRedirect("AdminModule/EditUsers.jsp?msg=An Administrator has
successfully been deleted.");
   }
 }
}
catch (Exception e)
{
   System.out.println(e.getLocalizedMessage());
}

// release resources
finally
{
   try
   {
      if (statement != null)
      {
          statement.close();
      }
   }
   catch (Exception e)
```

```
     {
     }
     try
     {
        if (connection != null)
        {
           connection.close();
        }
     }
     catch (Exception e)
     {
     }
  }
} // end deleteAdmin method

// updateAdmin method
public void updateAdmin(HttpServletRequest request, HttpServletResponse response, String
administratorID, String administratorUsername, String administratorPassword, String
administratorName, String administratorAddress, String administratorContactNumber, String
administratorEmail, String administratorAge, String administratorGender,String
administratorID2) throws IOException
{
   // server side fields validaion
   if (!administratorUsername.trim().equalsIgnoreCase("") &&
!administratorPassword.trim().equalsIgnoreCase("")
        && !administratorName.trim().equalsIgnoreCase("") &&
!administratorAddress.trim().equalsIgnoreCase("")
        && !administratorContactNumber.trim().equalsIgnoreCase("") &&
!administratorEmail.trim().equalsIgnoreCase("")
        && !administratorAge.trim().equalsIgnoreCase("") &&
!administratorGender.trim().equalsIgnoreCase(""))
   {
      try
      {
         int adminID = Integer.parseInt(administratorID);
         int adminID2 = Integer.parseInt(administratorID2);

         // connecting to database
         ConnectToDb connect = new ConnectToDb();
         connection = connect.connectToDb();

         // instantiating sql statement object
         statement = connection.createStatement();

         String  sql = "Select * from App.\"Administrator\" where
(\"administratorUsername\"='"+administratorUsername+"' or
```

```
\"administratorEmail\"='"+administratorEmail+"') and
(\"administratorID\"<>"+administratorID+")";
        resultSet = statement.executeQuery(sql);

        if(!resultSet.next())
        {
           if( adminID2 == 1 )
           {
              statement.executeUpdate("Update App.\"Administrator\" set
\"administratorUsername\"='" + administratorUsername + "', \"administratorPassword\" = '" +
administratorPassword + "', \"administratorName\" = '" + administratorName + "',
\"administratorAddress\" = '" + administratorAddress + "', \"administratorContactNumber\" = '"
+ administratorContactNumber + "', \"administratorEmail\" = '" + administratorEmail + "',
\"administratorAge\" = '" + administratorAge + "', \"administratorGender\" = '" +
administratorGender + "' where \"administratorID\" = '" + administratorID + "'");
              response.sendRedirect("AdminModule/EditUsers.jsp?usermsg=An Admin's
information has successfully been updated.");
           }
           else if(adminID != 1)
           {
              statement.executeUpdate("Update App.\"Administrator\" set
\"administratorUsername\"='" + administratorUsername + "', \"administratorPassword\" = '" +
administratorPassword + "', \"administratorName\" = '" + administratorName + "',
\"administratorAddress\" = '" + administratorAddress + "', \"administratorContactNumber\" = '"
+ administratorContactNumber + "', \"administratorEmail\" = '" + administratorEmail + "',
\"administratorAge\" = '" + administratorAge + "', \"administratorGender\" = '" +
administratorGender + "' where \"administratorID\" = '" + administratorID + "'");
              response.sendRedirect("AdminModule/EditUsers.jsp?usermsg=An Admin's
information has successfully been updated.");


           }
           else
           {
              response.sendRedirect("AdminModule/EditUsers.jsp?msg=Super Administrator
cannot be updated!");
           }

        }
        else
        {
           do
           {
              response.sendRedirect("AdminModule/EditUsers.jsp?msg=The entered Username
or email address is already taken. Please choose another Username or use another email
address!");
```

```
            } while(resultSet.next());
        }


        statement.close(); // closing the statement object
        connection.close(); // closing the connection

    }
    catch (Exception e)
    {
        System.out.println(e.getLocalizedMessage());
    }
}
else
{
    response.sendRedirect("AdminModule/EditUserView.jsp?msg=Please fill in all required
fields!");
}
} // end updateAdmin method

// deactivateAdmin method
public void deactivateAdmin(HttpServletRequest request, HttpServletResponse response,
String administratorID)
{
    String command = null;

    try
    {
        ConnectToDb connect = new ConnectToDb();
        connection = connect.connectToDb();

        // initializing an sql statement object
        statement = connection.createStatement();

        command = "Select * from App.\"Administrator\" where \"administratorID\"=" +
administratorID;
        resultSet = statement.executeQuery(command);

        if (resultSet.next())
        {
            String stringAdminID = resultSet.getString(1);
            int intAdminID = Integer.parseInt(stringAdminID);

            // Super Administrator cannot be deactivate
            if (intAdminID == 1)
            {
```

```
                    response.sendRedirect("AdminModule/EditUsers.jsp?msg=Super Administrator
cannot be deactivated!");
            }
            else
            {
                    command = "Update App.\"Administrator\" SET \"isActive\"='false' where
\"administratorID\"=" + administratorID;
                    statement.executeUpdate(command);
                    response.sendRedirect("AdminModule/EditUsers.jsp?msg=An Admin has been
deactivated.");
            }
        }

        statement.close();
        connection.close();
    }
    catch (Exception e)
    {
        System.err.println(e.getLocalizedMessage());
    }
} // end deactivateAdmin method

// activateAdmin method
public void activateAdmin(HttpServletRequest request, HttpServletResponse response, String
administratorID)
{
    try
    {
        ConnectToDb db = new ConnectToDb();
        connection = db.connectToDb();

        statement = connection.createStatement();

        String sql = "Update App.\"Administrator\" SET \"isActive\"='true' where
\"administratorID\"=" + administratorID;
        statement.executeUpdate(sql);
        response.sendRedirect("AdminModule/EditUsers.jsp?msg=An Admin has been
activated.");

        statement.close();
        connection.close();
    }
    catch (Exception e)
    {
        System.err.println(e.getLocalizedMessage());
    }
```

```
} // end activateAdmin method

// updateAuctioneer method
public void updateAuctioneer(HttpServletRequest request, HttpServletResponse response,
String auctioneerID, String auctioneerUsername, String auctioneerPassword, String
auctioneerName, String auctioneerAddress, String auctioneerContactNumber, String
auctioneerEmail, String auctioneerAge, String auctioneerGender) throws IOException
{
    // a server side check
    if (!auctioneerUsername.trim().equalsIgnoreCase("") &&
!auctioneerPassword.trim().equalsIgnoreCase("")
        && !auctioneerName.trim().equalsIgnoreCase("") &&
!auctioneerAddress.trim().equalsIgnoreCase("")
        && !auctioneerContactNumber.trim().equalsIgnoreCase("") &&
!auctioneerEmail.trim().equalsIgnoreCase("")
        && !auctioneerAge.trim().equalsIgnoreCase("") &&
!auctioneerGender.trim().equalsIgnoreCase(""))
    {
        String sql;

        try
        {
            ConnectToDb connect = new ConnectToDb();
            connection = connect.connectToDb();
            statement = connection.createStatement();


            sql = "Select * from App.\"Auctioneer\" where
(\"auctioneerUsername\"='"+auctioneerUsername+"' or
\"auctioneerEmail\"='"+auctioneerEmail+"') and (\"auctioneerID\"<>"+auctioneerID+")";
            resultSet = statement.executeQuery(sql);

            if(!resultSet.next())
            {
                statement.executeUpdate("Update App.\"Auctioneer\" set
\"auctioneerUsername\"='" + auctioneerUsername + "', \"auctioneerPassword\" = '" +
auctioneerPassword + "', \"auctioneerName\" = '" + auctioneerName + "', \"auctioneerAddress\"
= '" + auctioneerAddress + "', \"auctioneerContactNumber\" = '" + auctioneerContactNumber +
"', \"auctioneerEmail\" = '" + auctioneerEmail + "', \"auctioneerAge\" = '" + auctioneerAge + "',
\"auctioneerGender\" = '" + auctioneerGender + "' where \"auctioneerID\" = " + auctioneerID +
"");

                response.sendRedirect("AdminModule/EditAuctioneers.jsp?usermsg=An
Auctioneer's information has successfully been updated.");
            }
            else
```

```
      {
        do
        {
          response.sendRedirect("AdminModule/EditAuctioneers.jsp?msg=The entered
Username or email address is already taken. Please choose another Username or use another
email address!");

          } while(resultSet.next());

      }

        statement.close();
        connection.close();

      }
      catch (Exception e)
      {
        System.out.println(e.getLocalizedMessage());
      }
    }
    else
    {
      response.sendRedirect("AdminModule/EditAuctioneerView.jsp?msg=Please fill in all
required fields!");
    }
  } // end updateAuctioneer method

  // deactivateAuctioneer method
  public void deactivateAuctioneer(HttpServletRequest request, HttpServletResponse response,
String auctioneerID)
  {
    try
    {
      ConnectToDb connect = new ConnectToDb();
      connection = connect.connectToDb();

      // initializing an sql statement object
      statement = connection.createStatement();

      String command = "Update App.\"Auctioneer\" SET \"isActive\"=false where
\"auctioneerID\"=" + auctioneerID;
      statement.executeUpdate(command);
      response.sendRedirect("AdminModule/EditAuctioneers.jsp?msg=An Auctioneer has
been deactivated.");

      statement.clearBatch();
```

```
        statement.close();
        connection.close();
    }
    catch (Exception e)
    {
        System.err.println(e.getLocalizedMessage());
    }
} // end deactivateAuctioneer method

// activateAuctioneer method
public void activateAuctioneer(HttpServletRequest request, HttpServletResponse response,
String auctioneerID)
{
    try
    {
        ConnectToDb db = new ConnectToDb();
        connection = db.connectToDb();
        statement = connection.createStatement();

        String sql = "Update App.\"Auctioneer\" SET \"isActive\"=true where \"auctioneerID\"="
+ auctioneerID;
        statement.executeUpdate(sql);

        response.sendRedirect("AdminModule/EditAuctioneers.jsp?msg=An Auctioneer has
been activated.");

        statement.close();
        connection.close();
    }
    catch (Exception e)
    {
        System.err.println(e.getLocalizedMessage());
    }
} // end activateAuctioneer method

// updateBidder method
public void updateBidder(HttpServletRequest request, HttpServletResponse response, String
bidderID, String bidderUsername, String bidderPassword, String bidderName, String
bidderAddress, String bidderContactNumber, String bidderEmail, String bidderAge, String
bidderGender) throws IOException
{
    // a server side check
    if (!bidderUsername.trim().equalsIgnoreCase("") &&
!bidderPassword.trim().equalsIgnoreCase("")
            && !bidderName.trim().equalsIgnoreCase("") &&
!bidderAddress.trim().equalsIgnoreCase("")
```

```
                 && !biddercontactNumber.trim().equalsIgnoreCase("") &&
!bidderEmail.trim().equalsIgnoreCase("")
                 && !bidderAge.trim().equalsIgnoreCase("") &&
!bidderGender.trim().equalsIgnoreCase(""))
      {
            String sql;
            try
            {
                 ConnectToDb connect = new ConnectToDb();
                 connection = connect.connectToDb();

                 // instantiating sql statement object
                 statement=connection.createStatement();
                 sql = "Select * from App.\"Bidder\" where
(\"bidderUsername\"='"+bidderUsername+"' or \"bidderEmail\"='"+bidderEmail+"') and
(\"bidderID\"<>"+bidderID+")";
                 resultSet = statement.executeQuery(sql);

                 if(!resultSet.next())
                 {
                       statement.executeUpdate("Update App.\"Bidder\" set \"bidderUsername\"='" +
bidderUsername + "', \"bidderPassword\" = '" + bidderPassword + "', \"bidderName\" = '" +
bidderName + "', \"bidderAddress\" = '" + bidderAddress + "', \"bidderContactNumber\" = '" +
bidderContactNumber + "', \"bidderEmail\" = '" + bidderEmail + "', \"bidderAge\" = '" +
bidderAge + "', \"bidderGender\" = '" + bidderGender + "' where \"bidderID\" = " + bidderID +
"");

                       response.sendRedirect("AdminModule/EditBidders.jsp?usermsg=A Bidder's
information has successfully been updated.");
                 }
                 else
                 {
                       do
                       {
                             response.sendRedirect("AdminModule/EditBidders.jsp?msg=The entered
Username or email address is already taken. Please choose another Username or use another
email address!");

                       } while(resultSet.next());

                 }

                 statement.close();
                 connection.close();

      }
```

```
        catch (Exception es)
        {
          System.out.println(es.getLocalizedMessage());
        }
      }
      else
      {
        response.sendRedirect("AdminModule/EditBidderView.jsp?msg=Please fill in all
required fields!");
      }

    } // end updateBidder method

    // deactivateBidder method
    public void deactivateBidder(HttpServletRequest request, HttpServletResponse response,
String bidderID)
    {
        try
        {
          ConnectToDb connect = new ConnectToDb();
          connection = connect.connectToDb();

          // initializing an sql statement object
          statement = connection.createStatement();

          String command = "Update App.\"Bidder\" SET \"isActive\"=false where \"bidderID\"="
+ bidderID;
          statement.executeUpdate(command);

          response.sendRedirect("AdminModule/EditBidders.jsp?msg=A Bidder has been
deactivated.");

          statement.clearBatch();
          statement.close();
          connection.close();

        }
        catch (Exception e)
        {
          System.err.println(e.getLocalizedMessage());
        }
    } // end deactivateBidder method

    // activateBidder method
    public void activateBidder(HttpServletRequest request, HttpServletResponse response, String
bidderID)
```

```
{

    try
    {
        ConnectToDb db = new ConnectToDb();
        connection = db.connectToDb();

        statement = connection.createStatement();

        String sql = "Update App.\"Bidder\" SET \"isActive\"=true where \"bidderID\"=" +
bidderID;
        statement.executeUpdate(sql);

        response.sendRedirect("AdminModule/EditBidders.jsp?msg=A Bidder has been
activated.");

        statement.close();
        connection.close();
    }
    catch (Exception e)
    {
        System.err.println(e.getLocalizedMessage());
    }
    } // end activateBidder method
} // end class Admin

/*
 * Saudi eBay Project
 * Last Modified: Mon Nov 17, 2014 6:00 PM
 * The AdminLoginAction class is used to check whether or not the entered username and
password are empty
 * This class is used for Admins, Auctioneers, and Bidders
 */
// import statements
package org.saudiebay.adminmodule;
// class AdminLoginAction
public class AdminLoginAction{
    // authenticate method to return false if either username or password is left empty
    // Otherwise, it will return ture
    public boolean authenticate(String username, String password)
    {
        if (username.trim().equalsIgnoreCase("") || password.trim().equalsIgnoreCase(""))
            return false;
        return true;
    } // end authenticate method
} // end AdminLoginAction class
```

```
/*
 * Saudi eBay Project
 * Last Modified: Mon Nov 17, 2014 6:00 PM
 * The Auction class is used to start, end, and deactivate an auciton, and to award a bid
 * This class calls methods from class AuctionController
 */

package org.saudiebay.auctioneermodule;

// import statements
import java.io.IOException;
import java.io.PrintWriter;
import java.sql.Statement;
import javax.servlet.ServletException;
import javax.servlet.http.HttpServlet;
import javax.servlet.http.HttpServletRequest;
import javax.servlet.http.HttpServletResponse;

// class Auction
public class Auction extends HttpServlet
{
    // variables declaration
    private String productID;
    private String productOpenPrice;
    private String auctioneerID;
    private String categoryID;
    private String auctionStartDate;
    private String auctionEndDate;
    private String bidderID;
    private String auctionID;
    private String bidID;

    /**
     * Processes requests for both HTTP <code>GET</code> and <code>POST</code>
     * methods.
     *
     * @param request servlet request
     * @param response servlet response
     * @throws ServletException if a servlet-specific error occurs
     * @throws IOException if an I/O error occurs
     */

    // processRequest method
    protected void processRequest(HttpServletRequest request, HttpServletResponse response)
    throws ServletException, IOException
    {
```

```
response.setContentType("text/html;charset=UTF-8");

try (PrintWriter out = response.getWriter())
{
    AuctionController auctionController = new AuctionController();
    //Statement statement;

    if(request.getParameter("deactivateauction")!=null)
    {
        auctionID = request.getParameter("auctionID");
        auctionController.deactivateAuction(request, response, auctionID);
    }

    if (request.getParameter("startauction") != null)
    {
        String auctioneerUsername = request.getParameter("auctioneerUsername");

        productID = request.getParameter("productID");
        productOpenPrice = request.getParameter("productOpenPrice");
        auctioneerID = request.getParameter("auctioneerID");
        categoryID = request.getParameter("categoryID");
        auctionStartDate = request.getParameter("auctionStartDate");
        auctionEndDate = request.getParameter("auctionEndDate");

        auctionController.startAuction(request, response, productID, productOpenPrice,
auctioneerID, categoryID, auctionStartDate, auctionEndDate, auctioneerUsername);
    }

    if (request.getParameter("endauction") != null)
    {
        auctionID = request.getParameter("auctionID");
        auctionController.endAuction(request, response, auctionID);
    }

    if (request.getParameter("awardbid") != null)
    {
        productID = request.getParameter("productID");
        auctionID = request.getParameter("auctionID");
        bidderID = request.getParameter("bidderID");
        bidID = request.getParameter("bidID");

        auctionController.awardBids(request, response, auctionID, bidderID,bidID,productID);
    }
}
} // end proccessRequest method
```

```
// <editor-fold defaultstate="collapsed" desc="HttpServlet methods. Click on the + sign on the
left to edit the code.">
/**
 * Handles the HTTP <code>GET</code> method.
 *
 * @param request servlet request
 * @param response servlet response
 * @throws ServletException if a servlet-specific error occurs
 * @throws IOException if an I/O error occurs
 */
@Override
protected void doGet(HttpServletRequest request, HttpServletResponse response)
    throws ServletException, IOException {
  processRequest(request, response);
}

/**
 * Handles the HTTP <code>POST</code> method.
 *
 * @param request servlet request
 * @param response servlet response
 * @throws ServletException if a servlet-specific error occurs
 * @throws IOException if an I/O error occurs
 */
@Override
protected void doPost(HttpServletRequest request, HttpServletResponse response)
    throws ServletException, IOException {
  processRequest(request, response);
}

/**
 * Returns a short description of the servlet.
 *
 * @return a String containing servlet description
 */
@Override
public String getServletInfo() {
  return "Short description";
}// </editor-fold>

} // end class Auction
```

```
/*
 * Saudi eBay Project
 * Last Modified: Mon Nov 17, 2014 6:00 PM
 * The AuctionController class is used to start an auction, end an auction, deactivate an auction,
 and award a bid
 */

package org.saudiebay.auctioneermodule;
// import statements
import java.io.PrintWriter;
import java.sql.Connection;
import java.sql.ResultSet;
import java.sql.Statement;
import java.text.SimpleDateFormat;
import java.util.Calendar;
import java.util.Date;
import javax.servlet.http.HttpServletRequest;
import javax.servlet.http.HttpServletResponse;
import org.saudiebay.dbaccess.ConnectToDb;

// AuctionController class
public class AuctionController
{
    // variables declaration
    Connection connection;
    Statement statement;
    ResultSet resultSet;
    // startAuction method
    public void startAuction(HttpServletRequest request, HttpServletResponse response, String
productID, String productOpenPrice, String auctioneerID, String categoryID, String
auctionStartDate, String auctionEndDate,String auctioneerUsername)
    {
        if (!productID.trim().equalsIgnoreCase("") &&
!productOpenPrice.trim().equalsIgnoreCase("") && !auctioneerID.trim().equalsIgnoreCase("")
&& !auctionStartDate.trim().equalsIgnoreCase("") &&
!auctionEndDate.trim().equalsIgnoreCase(""))
        {
            try
            {
                long time = System.currentTimeMillis();
                Date todayDate = new Date(time);
                Date dateStart = new SimpleDateFormat("yyyy-MM-dd").parse(auctionStartDate);
                Date dateEnd = new SimpleDateFormat("yyyy-MM-dd").parse(auctionEndDate);

                Calendar cal1 = Calendar.getInstance();
                Calendar cal2 = Calendar.getInstance();
```

```
cal1.setTime(todayDate);
cal2.setTime(dateStart);

boolean sameDate = cal1.get(Calendar.YEAR) == cal2.get(Calendar.YEAR) &&
cal1.get(Calendar.DAY_OF_YEAR) == cal2.get(Calendar.DAY_OF_YEAR);

if(sameDate && dateEnd.after(dateStart))
{
    ConnectToDb connect = new ConnectToDb(); // connecting to the database
    connection = connect.connectToDb();

    statement = connection.createStatement();
    String command = "INSERT INTO
APP.\"Auction\"(\"productID\",\"auctioneerID\",\"auctioneerUsername\",\"auctionStartDate\",\"a
uctionEndDate\",\"isActive\",\"isAwarded\") VALUES(" + productID + "," + auctioneerID +
",'"+auctioneerUsername+"','" + auctionStartDate + "','" + auctionEndDate +
"',true,false)";//Other wise if it not already exists than create the query to insert it in database
    statement.executeUpdate(command); // executing the sql command

    response.sendRedirect("AuctioneerModule/MyAuctions.jsp");

    statement.close();
    connection.close();
}
else
{
    PrintWriter writer = response.getWriter();
    writer.write("Please make sure that start and end dates are correctly selected! Please
go back and check them.");
}

}
catch (Exception e) {
    e.printStackTrace();
}
}
} // end startAuction method

// endAuction method
public void endAuction(HttpServletRequest request, HttpServletResponse response,String
auctionID)
{
    if (!auctionID.trim().equalsIgnoreCase(""))
    {
        try
        {
```

```
        ConnectToDb connect = new ConnectToDb(); // connecting to the database
        connection = connect.connectToDb();

        statement = connection.createStatement();
        String command = "Delete from APP.\"Auction\" where \"auctionID\"=" + auctionID;
        statement.executeUpdate(command); // executing the sql command

        response.sendRedirect("AuctioneerModule/MyProducts.jsp");

        statement.close();
        connection.close();
    }
    catch (Exception e)
    {
        System.err.println(e.getLocalizedMessage());
    }
    }
    } // end endAuction method

    // awardBid method
    public void awardBids(HttpServletRequest request, HttpServletResponse response, String
    auctionID, String bidderID,String bidID,String productID)
    {
        String command = null;
        Statement stmt = null;

        try
        {
            ConnectToDb db = new ConnectToDb();
            connection = db.connectToDb();

            stmt = connection.createStatement();

            command = "Update App.\"Product\" SET \"isSold\"=true where \"productID\"=" +
    productID;
            stmt.executeUpdate(command);
            stmt.clearBatch();

            command = "Update App.\"Auction\" SET \"isActive\"=false where \"auctionID\"=" +
    auctionID;
            stmt.executeUpdate(command);
            stmt.clearBatch();

            command = "Update App.\"Auction\" SET \"isAwarded\"=true where \"auctionID\"=" +
    auctionID;
            stmt.executeUpdate(command);
```

```
stmt.clearBatch();

command = "Update App.\"Bid\" SET \"bidWinner\"='winner' where \"bidderID\"=" +
bidderID + "and \"bidID\"="+bidID;
stmt.executeUpdate(command);
stmt.clearBatch();

command = "INSERT INTO
APP.\"AuctionBidderStatus\"(\"auctionID\",\"bidderID\",\"status\") VALUES(" + auctionID +
"," + bidderID + ",'" + "awarded" + "')";
stmt.executeUpdate(command);
stmt.clearBatch();

response.sendRedirect("AuctioneerModule/AwardedBids.jsp");

stmt.close();
connection.close();
}
catch (Exception e)
{
    System.err.println(e.getLocalizedMessage());
}
} // end awardBid method

// method deactivateAuction
void deactivateAuction(HttpServletRequest request, HttpServletResponse response, String
auctionID)
{
    try
    {
        ConnectToDb db = new ConnectToDb();
        connection = db.connectToDb();
        statement = connection.createStatement();
        String command = "Update App.\"Auction\" SET \"isActive\"=false where
\"auctionID\"=" + auctionID;
        statement.executeUpdate(command);
        statement.clearBatch();

        response.sendRedirect("AdminModule/EditAuctions.jsp");
    }
    catch(Exception e)
    {
        System.out.println(e.getLocalizedMessage());
    }
} // end method deactivateAuction
} // end AuctionController class
```

```
/*
 * Saudi eBay Project
 * Last Modified: Mon Nov 17, 2014 6:00 PM
 * The Auctioneer class is used to to register a new Auctioneer in the Saudi_eBay database and
 to login as an Auctioneer
 */

package org.saudiebay.auctioneermodule;

// import statements
import java.io.IOException;
import java.sql.Connection;
import java.sql.ResultSet;
import java.sql.Statement;
import javax.servlet.ServletException;
import javax.servlet.http.HttpServlet;
import javax.servlet.http.HttpServletRequest;
import javax.servlet.http.HttpServletResponse;
import javax.servlet.http.HttpSession;
import org.saudiebay.adminmodule.AdminLoginAction;
import org.saudiebay.dbaccess.ConnectToDb;

// Auctioneer class
public class Auctioneer extends HttpServlet
{
    // variables decleration
    private ResultSet resultSet;
    private Connection connection;
    private Statement statement;
    private String auctioneerUsername;
    private String auctioneerPassword;
    private String auctioneerName;
    private String auctioneerAddress;
    private String auctioneerContactNumber;
    private String auctioneerEmail;
    private String auctioneerAge;
    private String auctioneerGender;

    /**
     * Processes requests for both HTTP <code>GET</code> and <code>POST</code>
     * methods.
     *
     * @param request servlet request
     * @param response servlet response
     * @throws ServletException if a servlet-specific error occurs
     * @throws IOException if an I/O error occurs
```

```
*/

// doGet method
@Override
protected void doGet(HttpServletRequest request, HttpServletResponse response) throws
ServletException, IOException
{
    response.setContentType("text/html;charset=UTF-8");

    if (request.getParameter("auctioneerlogin") != null)
    {
        auctioneerUsername = request.getParameter("auctioneerUsername");
        auctioneerPassword = request.getParameter("auctioneerPassword");

        doLogin(request, response, auctioneerUsername, auctioneerPassword);
    }

    if (request.getParameter("auctioneerregistration") != null)
    {
        auctioneerUsername = request.getParameter("auctioneerUsername");
        auctioneerPassword = request.getParameter("auctioneerPassword");
        auctioneerName = request.getParameter("auctioneerName");
        auctioneerAddress = request.getParameter("auctioneerAddress");
        auctioneerContactNumber = request.getParameter("auctioneerContactNumber");
        auctioneerEmail = request.getParameter("auctioneerEmail");
        auctioneerAge = request.getParameter("auctioneerAge");
        auctioneerGender = request.getParameter("auctioneerGender");

        registerAuctioneer(request, response, auctioneerUsername, auctioneerPassword,
auctioneerName, auctioneerAddress, auctioneerContactNumber, auctioneerEmail,
auctioneerAge, auctioneerGender);
    }
} // end doGet method

// doLogin method
public void doLogin(HttpServletRequest request, HttpServletResponse response, String
auctioneerUsername, String auctioneerPassword) throws IOException
{
    String userSessionID;
    String query = null;

    // creating an object of class AdminLoginAction
    AdminLoginAction adminLoginAction = new AdminLoginAction();

    try
    {
```

```
        ConnectToDb db = new ConnectToDb();
        connection = db.connectToDb();

        // calling auhtenticate method and passing username and password to make sure that they
both are not empty
        boolean result = adminLoginAction.authenticate(auctioneerUsername,
auctioneerPassword);

        if (result)
        {
            statement = connection.createStatement();
            query = "select * from APP.\"Auctioneer\" where \"auctioneerUsername\" = '" +
auctioneerUsername + "' and \"auctioneerPassword\"= '" + auctioneerPassword + "'";

            // executing the query and storing the returned resultset (result set is a complete table)
            resultSet = statement.executeQuery(query);

            if (resultSet.next())
            {
                query = "select * from APP.\"Auctioneer\" where \"auctioneerUsername\" = '" +
auctioneerUsername + "' and \"auctioneerPassword\"= '" + auctioneerPassword + "' and
\"isActive\"= true";

                // executing the query and storing the returned resultset
                resultSet = statement.executeQuery(query);

                if (resultSet.next())
                {
                    userSessionID = resultSet.getString(1);

                    // creating sessions
                    HttpSession httpSession = request.getSession(true);
                    httpSession.setAttribute("auctioneerID", userSessionID);

                    // if the username and password entered are matched with those in Auctioneer
table, the response will be redirected to AuctioneerPanel
                    response.sendRedirect("AuctioneerModule/AuctioneerPanel.jsp");

                }
                else
                {
                    response.sendRedirect("AuctioneerModule/AuctioneerLogin.jsp?error=Your
Username is Inactive. Please contact the Administrator via email.");
                }
            }
            else
```

```
        {
                response.sendRedirect("AuctioneerModule/AuctioneerLogin.jsp?error=Wrong
Username or Password. Please try again!");
        }
    }
    else
    {
            response.sendRedirect("AuctioneerModule/AuctioneerLogin.jsp?error=Please fill in all
required fields!");
        }
    }
    catch (Exception e)
    {
        System.err.println(e.getLocalizedMessage());
    }
} // end doLogin method

// method registerAuctioneer
public void registerAuctioneer(HttpServletRequest request, HttpServletResponse response,
String auctioneerUsername, String auctioneerPassword, String auctioneerName, String
auctioneerAddress, String auctioneerContactNumber, String auctioneerEmail, String
auctioneerAge, String auctioneerGender) throws IOException
{
    // a server side fields validation to make sure that feilds are not left empty
    if (!auctioneerUsername.trim().equalsIgnoreCase("") &&
!auctioneerPassword.trim().equalsIgnoreCase("") &&
!auctioneerName.trim().equalsIgnoreCase("") && !auctioneerEmail.trim().equalsIgnoreCase("")
    && !auctioneerAddress.trim().equalsIgnoreCase("") &&
!auctioneerContactNumber.trim().equalsIgnoreCase("") &&
!auctioneerAge.trim().equalsIgnoreCase("") && !auctioneerGender.trim().equalsIgnoreCase(""))
    {
        try
        {
            // connecting to the database
            ConnectToDb connect = new ConnectToDb();
            connection = connect.connectToDb();

            // initializing sql statement object
            statement = connection.createStatement();

            // a query to check if the entered username or email already exist in the database
            String query = "select * from APP.\"Auctioneer\" where \"auctioneerUsername\"='" +
auctioneerUsername + "' or \"auctioneerEmail\"='" + auctioneerEmail + "'";

            // executing the query
            resultSet = statement.executeQuery(query);
```

```
          // if the username or the email already exist in the Auctioneer table
          if (resultSet.next())
          {
              // sending the redirect to the same Registration.jsp page with the message that the
username or the email already exist
              response.sendRedirect("AuctioneerModule/Registration.jsp?msg=The entered
Username or email address is already taken. Please choose another Username or use another
email address!");
          }
          else
          {
              String command = "INSERT INTO
APP.\"Auctioneer\"(\"auctioneerUsername\",\"auctioneerPassword\",\"auctioneerName\",\"auctio
neerAddress\",\"auctioneerContactNumber\",\"auctioneerEmail\",\"auctioneerAge\",\"auctioneer
Gender\",\"isActive\") VALUES('" + auctioneerUsername + "','" + auctioneerPassword + "','" +
auctioneerName + "','" + auctioneerAddress + "','" + auctioneerContactNumber + "','" +
auctioneerEmail + "','" + auctioneerAge + "','" + auctioneerGender + "',true)";

              // executing the sql command
              statement.executeUpdate(command);

              response.sendRedirect("AuctioneerModule/AuctioneerLogin.jsp?error=A new
Auctioneer has successfully been created.");
          }
      }
      catch (Exception e)
      {
          System.err.println(e.getLocalizedMessage());
      }

      // release resources
      finally
      {
          try
          {
              if (resultSet != null)
              {
                  resultSet.close();
              }
          }
          catch (Exception e)
          {
          }

          try
```

```
        {
           if (statement != null)
           {
              statement.close();
           }
        }
        catch (Exception e)
        {
        }

        try
        {
           if (connection != null)
           {
              connection.close();
           }
        }
        catch (Exception e)
        {
        }
     }
  }
  else
  {
     response.sendRedirect("AuctioneerModule/Registration.jsp?msg=Please fill in all
required fields!");
  }
  } // end registerAuctioneer method
} // end Auctioneer class
```

```
/*
 * Saudi eBay Project
 * Last Modified: Mon Nov 17, 2014 6:00 PM
 * The Product class is used to add products to the Saudi_eBay database by Auctioneer
 * and keep tracking of these products by their images' paths.
 * It also provides delete and update products features
 */


package org.saudiebay.auctioneermodule;

// import statements
import java.io.File;
import java.io.IOException;
import java.sql.Connection;
import java.sql.ResultSet;
import java.sql.Statement;
import java.util.Iterator;
import java.util.List;
import javax.servlet.ServletException;
import javax.servlet.http.HttpServlet;
import javax.servlet.http.HttpServletRequest;
import javax.servlet.http.HttpServletResponse;
import org.apache.commons.fileupload.FileItem;
import org.apache.commons.fileupload.FileItemFactory;
import org.apache.commons.fileupload.disk.DiskFileItemFactory;
import org.apache.commons.fileupload.servlet.ServletFileUpload;
import org.saudiebay.dbaccess.ConnectToDb;

// Product class
public class Product extends HttpServlet
{
    // variables decleration
    private Connection connection;
    private Statement statement;
    private ResultSet resultSet;
    private String categoryID;
    private String auctioneerID;
    private String productName;
    private String productDescription;
    private String productOpenPrice;

    /**
     * Processes requests for both HTTP <code>GET</code> and <code>POST</code>
     * methods.
     *
     * @param request servlet request
```

```
* @param response servlet response
* @throws ServletException if a servlet-specific error occurs
* @throws IOException if an I/O error occurs
*/

// method doPost
@Override
protected void doPost(HttpServletRequest request, HttpServletResponse response) throws
ServletException, IOException
{
    String root = null; // Path variable for storing the path of the image uploaded on server, so
that image can be retrieved on other pages through that path
    response.setContentType("text/html;charset=UTF-8"); // setting the response content type to
html
    root = getServletContext().getRealPath("/uploads"); // storing the absolute path of the
project on the server

    if (request.getParameter("deleteproduct") != null)
    {
        String productID = request.getParameter("productID");
        deleteProduct(request,response,productID);
    }

    else if (request.getParameter("updateproduct") != null)
    {
        String productID = request.getParameter("productID");
        productName = request.getParameter("productName");
        productDescription = request.getParameter("productDescription");
        productOpenPrice = request.getParameter("productOpenPrice");
        updateProduct(request, response, productID, productName, productDescription,
productOpenPrice);
    }
    else
    {
        addNewProduct(request, response, root); // calling a method for adding new product
    }
} // end method doPost

/**
*
* @param request
* @param response
* @param root
*/

// addNewProduct method
```

```
public void addNewProduct(HttpServletRequest request, HttpServletResponse response,
String root)
{
    FileItem item = null; // FileItem is used to retrieve the form fields when then MultiPart
content is submitted from form in that case both name attribute do not work
    File path = null; // path for image file
    String fileName = null; // filename is actually a image file name that is uploaded

    boolean isMultipart = ServletFileUpload.isMultipartContent(request); // checking if the
form submitted is multipart(contains file upload(image upload in our case))

    if (isMultipart) // if multipart then it is true
    {
        FileItemFactory factory = new DiskFileItemFactory(); // it is used to retrieve the
items/form fields with name attribute
        ServletFileUpload upload = new ServletFileUpload(factory); // for file uploading

        try
        {
            List items = upload.parseRequest(request); // checking the request type, post in our
case
            Iterator iterator = items.iterator(); // iterator iterates through FileItem items that
contains form field to retrieve each form field one by one

            while (iterator.hasNext()) // continue to loop to FileItem object to retrieve all form
fields
            {
                item = (FileItem) iterator.next(); // moving the cursor from 0 position to 1

                if (item.isFormField()) // checking if its a form field
                {
                    String name = item.getFieldName();

                    if (name.equals("auctioneerID")) // checking the input field with auctioneerID
name attribute
                    {
                        auctioneerID = item.getString(); // retrieving form field and storing it in
auctioneerID
                    }
                    else if (name.equals("productName"))
                    {
                        productName = item.getString();
                    }
                    else if (name.equals("categoryID"))
                    {
                        categoryID = item.getString();
```

```
                }
                else if (name.equals("productOpenPrice"))
                {
                    productOpenPrice = item.getString();
                }
                else if (name.equals("productDescription"))
                {
                    productDescription = item.getString();
                }
            }

        } // end while

        // a server side fields validation to make sure that fields are not empty
        if (!productName.trim().equalsIgnoreCase("") &&
!categoryID.trim().equalsIgnoreCase("") && !productOpenPrice.trim().equalsIgnoreCase("")
&& !productDescription.trim().equalsIgnoreCase(""))//Checking if all fields are filled in product
upload form
        {
            try
            {
                // connecting to the database
                ConnectToDb connect = new ConnectToDb(); // connecting to database
                connection = connect.connectToDb();

                // initializing sql statement object
                statement = connection.createStatement(); // creating a sql statement object

                if (!item.isFormField())
                {
                    fileName = item.getName(); // getting the path on uploaded image
                    path = new File(root);
                    if (!path.exists())
                    {
                        boolean status = path.mkdirs();
                    }

                    File uploadedFile = new File(path + "/" + fileName); // if path exists on the
current file system, it will upload the file
                    item.write(uploadedFile);
                }

                String command = "INSERT INTO
APP.\"Product\"(\"categoryID\",\"auctioneerID\",\"productName\",\"productDescription\",\"prod
uctOpenPrice\",\"path\",\"isSold\") VALUES(" + categoryID + "," + auctioneerID + ",'" +
productName + "','" + productDescription + "'," + productOpenPrice + ",'" + root + "\\" +
```

```
fileName + "',false)";
        statement.executeUpdate(command); // executing the query and storing path and
other form fields of item upload


response.sendRedirect("AuctioneerModule/ProductAddSummary.jsp?categoryID=" +
categoryID + "&auctioneerID=" + auctioneerID + "&productName=" + productName +
"&productDescription=" + productDescription + "&productOpenPrice=" + productOpenPrice +
"&path=" + path + "\\" + "&filename=" + fileName);

        }
        catch (Exception e)
        {
            System.err.println(e.getLocalizedMessage());
        }

        // release resources
        finally
        {
            try
            {
                if (resultSet != null)
                {
                    resultSet.close();
                }
            }
            catch (Exception e)
            {
            }

            try
            {
                if (statement != null)
                {
                    statement.close();
                }
            }
            catch (Exception e)
            {
            }

            try
            {
                if (connection != null)
                {
                    connection.close();
```

```
                    }
                   }
                  catch (Exception e)
                  {
                  }
                }
              }
              else
              {
                  response.sendRedirect("AuctioneerModule/UploadProduct.jsp?error=Please fill in
all required fields!");
              }
          }
          catch (Exception e)
          {
              e.printStackTrace();
          }
        }
    } // end addNewProduct method

    // updateProduct method
    public void updateProduct(HttpServletRequest request, HttpServletResponse response, String
productID, String productName, String productDescription, String productOpenPrice) throws
IOException
    {
        if (!productID.trim().equalsIgnoreCase("") && !productName.trim().equalsIgnoreCase("")
&& !productDescription.trim().equalsIgnoreCase("") &&
!productOpenPrice.trim().equalsIgnoreCase(""))
        {
            try
            {
                // connecting to database
                ConnectToDb connect = new ConnectToDb();
                connection = connect.connectToDb();

                statement = connection.createStatement();
                String sql = "Select * from App.\"Auction\" where \"productID\"= "+ productID;
                resultSet = statement.executeQuery(sql);
                boolean isActive = false;

                if(resultSet.next())
                {
                    isActive = resultSet.getBoolean(7);
                }

                System.out.println(isActive);
```

```
        if(!isActive)
        {
            statement.executeUpdate("Update App.\"Product\" set \"productName\"='" +
productName + "', \"productOpenPrice\" = " + productOpenPrice + ", \"productDescription\" = '"
+ productDescription + "' where \"productID\" = " + productID + "");
            response.sendRedirect("AuctioneerModule/MyProducts.jsp");
        }
        else
        {
            response.sendRedirect("AuctioneerModule/MyProducts.jsp?msg=A product's details
cannot be changed while an auction is active! Please contact the Administrator via email if you
have any problem.");
        }

        statement.close(); // closing the statement object
        connection.close(); // closing the connection
    }
    catch (Exception e)
    {
        System.out.println(e.getLocalizedMessage());
    }
}
else
{
    response.sendRedirect("AuctioneerModule/MyProducts.jsp");
}
} // end updateProduct method

// deleteProduct method
private void deleteProduct(HttpServletRequest request, HttpServletResponse response, String
productID)
{
    try
    {
        // connecting to database
        ConnectToDb connect = new ConnectToDb();
        connection = connect.connectToDb();
        statement = connection.createStatement();

        String sql = "Select * from App.\"Auction\" where \"productID\"= "+ productID;
        resultSet = statement.executeQuery(sql);

        boolean isActive = false;

        if(resultSet.next())
```

```
    {
        isActive = resultSet.getBoolean(7);
    }

    System.out.println(isActive);

    if(!isActive)
    {
        statement = connection.createStatement();
        statement.executeUpdate("Delete  from App.\"Product\" where \"productID\"=" +
productID );

        response.sendRedirect("AuctioneerModule/MyProducts.jsp");
    }
    else
    {
        response.sendRedirect("AuctioneerModule/MyProducts.jsp?msg=A product cannot be
deleted while an auction is active! Please contact the Administrator via email if you have any
problem.");
    }
    }
    catch(Exception e)
    {
        System.out.println(e.getLocalizedMessage());
    }
    } // end deleteProduct method
} // end Product class
```

```
/*
 * Saudi eBay Project
 * Last Modified: Mon Nov 17, 2014 6:00 PM
 * The Bid class is used to place a bid using an object from class Bidder
 */


package org.saudiebay.biddermodule;

// import statements
import java.io.IOException;
import javax.servlet.ServletException;
import javax.servlet.http.HttpServlet;
import javax.servlet.http.HttpServletRequest;
import javax.servlet.http.HttpServletResponse;

// class Bid
public class Bid extends HttpServlet
{
    // variables declaration
    String auctionID;
    String bidderID;
    String bidderUsername;
    String auctioneerID;
    String auctioneerUsername;
    String bidDate;
    String bidTime;
    String bidPrice;
    String highestBidPrice;
    String productOpenPrice;
    String productID;

    /**
     * Processes requests for both HTTP <code>GET</code> and <code>POST</code>
     * methods.
     *
     * @param request servlet request
     * @param response servlet response
     * @throws ServletException if a servlet-specific error occurs
     * @throws IOException if an I/O error occurs
     */
    // <editor-fold defaultstate="collapsed" desc="HttpServlet methods. Click on the + sign on the
left to edit the code.">
    /**
     * Handles the HTTP <code>GET</code> method.
     *
     * @param request servlet request
```

```
 * @param response servlet response
 * @throws ServletException if a servlet-specific error occurs
 * @throws IOException if an I/O error occurs
 */

// doGet method
@Override
protected void doGet(HttpServletRequest request, HttpServletResponse response) throws
ServletException, IOException
{
    bidderUsername = request.getParameter("bidderUsername");
    auctionID = request.getParameter("auctionID");
    bidderID = request.getParameter("bidderID");
    auctioneerID = request.getParameter("auctioneerID");
    bidDate = request.getParameter("bidDate");
    bidTime = request.getParameter("bidTime");
    bidPrice = request.getParameter("bidPrice");
    highestBidPrice = request.getParameter("highestbidprice");
    productOpenPrice = request.getParameter("productOpenPrice");
    productID = request.getParameter("productID");
    auctioneerUsername = request.getParameter("auctioneerUsername");

    // place a bid
    Bidder bidder = new Bidder();
    bidder.placeBid(request, response, productID, auctionID, bidderID, auctioneerID, bidDate,
bidTime, bidPrice, highestBidPrice, productOpenPrice, bidderUsername, auctioneerUsername);
    } // end method doGet
} // end class Bid
```

```
/*
 * Saudi eBay Project
 * Last Modified: Mon Nov 17, 2014 6:00 PM
 * The Bidder class is used to register a new bidder in the database, to login as a Bidder,
 * and to place a bid on a product.
 */

package org.saudiebay.biddermodule;

// import statements
import java.io.IOException;
import java.sql.Connection;
import java.sql.ResultSet;
import java.sql.Statement;
import javax.servlet.ServletException;
import javax.servlet.http.HttpServlet;
import javax.servlet.http.HttpServletRequest;
import javax.servlet.http.HttpServletResponse;
import javax.servlet.http.HttpSession;
import org.saudiebay.adminmodule.AdminLoginAction;
import org.saudiebay.dbaccess.ConnectToDb;

// Bidder class
public class Bidder extends HttpServlet
{

    // variables declaration
    private Connection connection;
    private Statement statement;
    private ResultSet resultSet;

    private String bidderUsername;
    private String bidderPassword;
    private String bidderName;
    private String bidderAddress;
    private String bidderContactNumber;
    private String bidderEmail;
    private String bidderAge;
    private String bidderGender;

    /**
     * Processes requests for both HTTP <code>GET</code> and <code>POST</code>
     * methods.
     *
     * @param request servlet request
     * @param response servlet response
```

```
    * @throws ServletException if a servlet-specific error occurs
    * @throws IOException if an I/O error occurs
    */

    // doGet method
    @Override
    protected void doGet(HttpServletRequest request, HttpServletResponse response) throws
ServletException, IOException
    {
        response.setContentType("text/html;charset=UTF-8");

        if (request.getParameter("bidderlogin") != null)
        {
            bidderUsername = request.getParameter("bidderUsername");
            bidderPassword = request.getParameter("bidderPassword");

            doLogin(request, response, bidderUsername, bidderPassword);
        }

        if (request.getParameter("bidderregistration") != null)
        {
            bidderUsername = request.getParameter("bidderUsername");
            bidderPassword = request.getParameter("bidderPassword");
            bidderName = request.getParameter("bidderName");
            bidderAddress = request.getParameter("bidderAddress");
            bidderContactNumber = request.getParameter("bidderContactNumber");
            bidderEmail = request.getParameter("bidderEmail");
            bidderAge = request.getParameter("bidderAge");
            bidderGender = request.getParameter("bidderGender");
            registerBidder(request, response, bidderUsername, bidderPassword, bidderName,
bidderAddress, bidderContactNumber, bidderEmail, bidderAge, bidderGender);
        }
    } // end doGet method

    // doLogin method
    public void doLogin(HttpServletRequest request, HttpServletResponse response, String
bidderUsername, String bidderPassword) throws IOException
    {
        // creating an object of class AdminLoginAction
        AdminLoginAction adminLoginAction = new AdminLoginAction();

        // calling auhtenticate method and passing username and password to make sure that they
both are not empty
        boolean result = adminLoginAction.authenticate(bidderUsername, bidderPassword);

        if (result)
```

```
{
     String userSessionID;

     try
     {
          // connecting to the database
          ConnectToDb db = new ConnectToDb();
          connection = db.connectToDb();

          // creating the sql query object
          statement = connection.createStatement();
          String query = "select * from APP.\"Bidder\" where \"bidderUsername\" = '" +
bidderUsername + "' and \"bidderPassword\"= '" + bidderPassword + "'";

          // executing the query and storing the returned resultset (result set is a complete table)
          resultSet = statement.executeQuery(query);

          if (resultSet.next())
          {
               // creating another sql query object
               query = "select * from APP.\"Bidder\" where \"bidderUsername\" = '" +
bidderUsername + "' and \"bidderPassword\"= '" + bidderPassword + "' and \"isActive\"= true";

               // executing the query and storing the returned resultset
               resultSet = statement.executeQuery(query);

               if (resultSet.next())
               {
                    userSessionID = resultSet.getString(1); // retrieving BidderID from Bidder table

                    // creating a session
                    HttpSession httpSession = request.getSession(true);
                    httpSession.setAttribute("bidderID", userSessionID);

                    // if the username and password entered are matched with those in table, the
response will be redirected to BidderPanel page
                         response.sendRedirect("BidderModule/BidderPanel.jsp");
               }
               else
               {
                    response.sendRedirect("BidderModule/BidderLogin.jsp?error=Your Username is
Inactive. Please contact the Administrator via email.");

               }
          }
          else
```

```
            {
                response.sendRedirect("BidderModule/BidderLogin.jsp?error=Wrong Username or
        Password. Please try again!");
            }
        }
        catch (Exception e)
        {
            System.err.println(e.getLocalizedMessage());
        }
    }
    else
    {
        response.sendRedirect("BidderModule/BidderLogin.jsp?error=Please fill in all required
fields");
    }
    } // end doLogin method

    // registerBidder method
    public void registerBidder(HttpServletRequest request, HttpServletResponse response, String
    bidderUsername, String bidderPassword, String bidderName, String bidderAddress, String
    bidderContactNumber, String bidderEmail, String bidderAge, String bidderGender) throws
    IOException
    {
        // a server side fields validation to make sure that feilds are not left empty
        if (!bidderUsername.trim().equalsIgnoreCase("") &&
    !bidderPassword.trim().equalsIgnoreCase("") && !bidderEmail.trim().equalsIgnoreCase("")
            && !bidderName.trim().equalsIgnoreCase("") &&
    !bidderAddress.trim().equalsIgnoreCase("") &&
    !bidderContactNumber.trim().equalsIgnoreCase("")
            && !bidderAge.trim().equalsIgnoreCase("") &&
    !bidderGender.trim().equalsIgnoreCase(""))
        {
            try
            {
                // connecting to the database
                ConnectToDb connect = new ConnectToDb();
                connection = connect.connectToDb();

                // initializing sql statement object
                statement = connection.createStatement();

                // a query to check if the entered username or email already exist in the database
                String query = "select * from APP.\"Bidder\" where \"bidderEmail\"='" + bidderEmail
    + "' or \"bidderUsername\" ='" + bidderUsername + "'";

                // executing the query
```

```
        resultSet = statement.executeQuery(query);

        // if the username or the email already exist in the Bidder table
        if (resultSet.next())
        {
            // sending the redirect to the same Registration.jsp page with the message that the
username or the email already exist
            response.sendRedirect("BidderModule/Registration.jsp?msg=The entered Username
or email address is already taken. Please choose another Username or use another email
address!");
        }
        else
        {
            String command = "INSERT INTO
APP.\"Bidder\"(\"bidderUsername\",\"bidderPassword\",\"bidderName\",\"bidderAddress\",\"bid
derContactNumber\",\"bidderEmail\",\"bidderAge\",\"bidderGender\", \"isActive\") VALUES('"
+ bidderUsername + "','" + bidderPassword + "','" + bidderName + "','" + bidderAddress + "','" +
bidderContactNumber + "','" + bidderEmail + "','" + bidderAge + "','" + bidderGender + "',true)";
            statement.executeUpdate(command);

            // sending the redirect to the BidderLogin.jsp page with the message that A new
Bidder has successfully been created.
            response.sendRedirect("BidderModule/BidderLogin.jsp?error=A new Bidder has
successfully been created.");
        }

    }
    catch (Exception e)
    {
        System.err.println(e.getLocalizedMessage());
    }

    // release resources
    finally
    {
        try
        {
            if (resultSet != null)
            {
                resultSet.close();
            }
        }
        catch (Exception e)
        {
        }
```

```
     try
     {
        if (statement != null)
        {
           statement.close();
        }
     }
     catch (Exception e)
     {
     }

     try
     {
        if (connection != null)
        {
           connection.close();
        }
     }
     catch (Exception e)
     {
     }
   }
   else
   {
      response.sendRedirect("BidderModule/Registration.jsp?msg=Please fill in all required
fields!");
   }
} // end registerBidder method

// placeBid method
public void placeBid(HttpServletRequest request, HttpServletResponse response, String
productID, String auctionID, String bidderID, String auctioneerID, String bidDate, String
bidTime, String bidPrice, String highestBidPrice, String productOpenPrice,String
bidderUsername,String auctioneerUsername)
{
   String command = null;

   int productOpenPriceInt = Integer.parseInt(productOpenPrice);
   int highestBidPriceInt = Integer.parseInt(highestBidPrice);

   // if there is no bid yet
   if (highestBidPriceInt == 0)
   {
      highestBidPriceInt = productOpenPriceInt;
   }
```

```
try
{
    int bidPriceInt = Integer.parseInt(bidPrice);

    // a check to make sure that the new bidder price is higher than the highest bid price or
the ProductOpenPrice whichever is higher
    if (bidPriceInt > highestBidPriceInt)
    {
        // connecting to the database
        ConnectToDb connect = new ConnectToDb();
        connection = connect.connectToDb();

        statement = connection.createStatement();
        resultSet = statement.executeQuery("SELECT  *  FROM App.\"Bid\" where
\"auctionID\"="+auctionID+" ORDER BY \"bidWinner\" DESC FETCH FIRST ROW ONLY
");

        String bidderid = null;

        if (!resultSet.next())
        {
            resultSet.clearWarnings();
            statement.clearBatch();
            statement = connection.createStatement();

            command = "INSERT INTO
APP.\"Bid\"(\"auctionID\",\"bidderID\",\"auctioneerID\",\"productID\",\"bidderUsername\",\"auc
tioneerUsername\",\"bidDate\",\"bidTime\",\"bidPrice\") VALUES(" + auctionID + "," +
bidderID + "," + auctioneerID + "," + productID +
",'"+bidderUsername+"','"+auctioneerUsername+"','" + bidDate + "','" + bidTime + "'," +
bidPrice + ")";
            statement.executeUpdate(command); // executing the sql command
            statement.clearBatch();
            response.sendRedirect("BidderModule/MyBids.jsp"); // sending the redirect to the
MyBids.jsp page
        }
        else
        {
            bidderid = resultSet.getString("bidderID");

            int bidderidInt = Integer.parseInt(bidderid);
            int bidderIDInt = Integer.parseInt(bidderID);

            if (bidderidInt == bidderIDInt)
            {
```

```
                response.sendRedirect("BidderModule/PlaceBidError.jsp?msg=You cannot place
consecutive bids!");
            }
            else
            {
                statement = connection.createStatement();
                command = "INSERT INTO
APP.\"Bid\"(\"auctionID\",\"bidderID\",\"auctioneerID\",\"productID\",\"bidderUsername\",\"auc
tioneerUsername\",\"bidDate\",\"bidTime\",\"bidPrice\") VALUES(" + auctionID + "," +
bidderID + "," + auctioneerID + "," + productID +
",'"+bidderUsername+"','"+auctioneerUsername+"','" + bidDate + "','" + bidTime + "'," +
bidPrice + ")";
                statement.executeUpdate(command); // executing the sql command
                response.sendRedirect("BidderModule/MyBids.jsp"); // sending the redirect to the
MyBids.jsp page
            }
        }

        // release resources
        statement.close();
        connection.close();
    }
    else
    {
        response.sendRedirect("BidderModule/PlaceBidError.jsp?msg=Your bid MUST be
greater than the open price and the highest bid! Please go back to check them.");

    }
    }
    catch (Exception e)
    {
        System.out.println(e.getLocalizedMessage());
    }
    } // end placeBid method
} // end Bidder class
```